PATHS IN SOLITUDE

For Benedict

Eve Baker

PATHS IN SOLITUDE

ST PAULS

Cover: photo by Egidio Zanchin; graphics AGAM, Madonna dell'Olmo
(Cuneo), Italy

ST PAULS
Middlegreen, Slough SL3 6BT, United Kingdom
Moyglare Road, Maynooth, Co. Kildare, Ireland

© ST PAULS (UK) 1995

ISBN 085439 513 X

Set by TuKan, High Wycombe

Printed by Biddles Ltd, Guildford

ST PAULS is an activity of the priests and brothers of the Society of St Paul
who proclaim the Gospel through the media of social communication

Contents

Introduction

Solitude today is hard to find. The mountains, once places of solitude, have become the playgrounds of many. City culture has become the dominant one and people are never comfortable unless they are in a crowd. Solitude and silence are both a threat and a reproach. The problems of today, war, poverty, famine and environmental pollution press us urgently towards the creation of a more just and stable society and a sustainable universe. The religious task today is seen as the creation of community, in the hope that we may learn to live together in peace in our overpopulated world.

There are many people who live in a solitary way through circumstance, occupation, sickness or old age. Their solitude is not necessarily a welcome experience; it can be felt as loneliness or isolation from human contacts. For such people solitude is an experience of bitterness, underlined by modern sociological theory which, like the current fashion in spirituality, works with a model of togetherness. The spirituality of fifty years ago, with its medieval emphasis upon the saving of one's own soul, has been replaced by one where the important thing is to save everyone else from their own misfortune, from poverty, from maladjustment. The solitary person, according to this model, is one who is alienated from the values of society. The medical model of isolation, generally accepted, leads us to suppose that that which is cut off is deviant, an aberration. Those who are solitary are sick, deprived and unfortunate.

And yet, it would seem, solitude has never been more sought after. It is not just the psychological pressures of urban living, giving rise to a desire to "get away from it all" that are behind this search. Most people nowadays have far more leisure time than our ancestors ever knew; refreshment and changes of scene are part of the pattern of modern living. The idea of holiday has its root in the Jewish institution of Sabbath, the regular day when burdens are put down, the rest from daily care. Today's weekend with its frenzied activity does not have the same restorative effect. The pleasure is there; it is the peace which is missing.

But the retreat movement is thriving; people are seeking something which is missing from their daily lives, silence and solitude. Even religious communities, where one would expect to find more silence and solitude than in other places, now have one or two caravans hidden away in the woods. This search for exterior solitude reflects the search for inner solitude which an increasing number of people are feeling called to. This growing movement would seem to be running counter to the current theologies which work with a picture of an immanent God, one who is to be found in other people, images of the human incarnation of Christ. These models have replaced the earlier ones of a God above the world, the divine ruler who was reflected in hierarchy and monarchy as human institutions, images which nowadays have become empty of real meaning. The real power which these old figures were once meant to encapsulate has now of course moved from them to faceless international corporations.

Today's search for solitude is a search for God who is divinely other, who draws us into the mystery of God's being, beyond ourselves. Silence and solitude point towards the unknown, that which is beyond our daily experience of the noise and busyness of the modern world. To be solitary is not to escape from real life but to be aware of the mystery which is part of human life. The whole concept of what we mean by being human involves the dimension of mystery. The modern scientific world view seeks to discount this element of mystery in human life; in practice modern medicine treats us all as a collection of bodies in varying stages of decay which like machines must be patched and repaired to be made fully functional. Psychological medicine treats aspects of human behaviour with the intention of returning people to 'normal'. Norms are of course statistical fictions; they nevertheless form the boundaries of social acceptability, the Procrustean bed where people are stretched or shortened to fit.

If the element of mystery is removed from human life we are constrained within the bounds of human knowledge, the sphere of the specialist where, as the popular definition has it, more and more is known about less and less. By means of knowledge we keep mystery at bay and remove the threat which is posed to our being. The experts guard the world and preserve it from the risk of not-being. The expert is the one who knows more than most.

Knowledge, in the sense that we understand it in the West, is power. Knowledge structures are the means by which we place ourselves in the world and gain power over the anxieties of existence. By this means we take objects into ourselves, tame them, and make them tools of our endeavour. Western civilization has been based on this idea of domination, of humankind being the centre and pivot of the universe, man being the measure of all things. In the age of the computer total control of all knowledge seems within our grasp. We have come a long way from Columbus whose friends sought to dissuade him from moving beyond the boundaries of the known world lest he fall off the edge into the abyss of nothingness.

Yet it is the profound mystery of human life that makes us more than a mere problem in social or medical engineering. Our beginning and our end, our birth and our dying, are mysterious occurrences, as we become aware through observing other people being born or dying. It is the whole element of mystery that is addressed by religion, which does not approach it primarily by means of analysis or reduction (although both these methods and others have been present in western religion) but by reverence or worship, an acknowledgement of the mystery beyond knowledge.

The language of mystery is wisdom, not scientific dis-

9

course. It is the tragedy of the western Church that it has put its faith more in *scientia*, sure knowledge, than in *sapientia*, wisdom. *Scientia* seeks to push back the boundaries of mystery, *sapientia* seeks to make the mystery present. This is the function of liturgy, which should never be reduced to the level of mere human concerns. The Orthodox Churches, with their iconostases, have placed supreme emphasis upon the element of mystery in their liturgy, which is perhaps the secret of their present appeal for western seekers. Western liturgies, in their reforms of the last twenty years have sought for relevance at the expense of mystery. Perhaps it is now time to recruit a few poets to reformulate the language of mystery. The profound mystery of God moves like a shadow beyond the limits of prosaic speech. As in music, the silences of the liturgy provide space for God.

In silence and solitude one is drawn to encounter the mystery of God. One cannot encompass the mystery in words, or like Jacob at the ford (Gen 32:27) seek to know its name to have power over it. It is beyond comprehension, yet it has the power to draw one onward, the wholly other which searches out our whole being. This silence and solitude may be something only intermittently encountered, an experience which sometimes presses upon us, or it can be something chosen which may make demands upon our life. One becomes solitary when one says yes to these demands.

The solitary is the bearer of the future, of that which is not yet born, of the mystery which lies beyond the circle of lamplight or the edge of the known world. There are some who make raids into this unknown world of mystery and who come back bearing artefacts. These are the creative artists, the poets who offer us their vision of the mystery. Orpheus, the legendary poet and musician, is depicted as one who has power over the mystery and the natural world, charming the wild beasts, drawing trees and rocks from their places and stopping rivers in their courses. But there are also those who make solitude their home, who travel further into the inner desert, from which they bring back few artefacts. These are the contemplatives, those who are drawn into the heart of the mystery. Contemplatives have no function and no ministry. They are in the world as a fish is in the sea, to use Catherine of Siena's phrase, as part of the mystery. That they are necessary is proved by the fact that they exist in all religious traditions. Contemplatives are not as a rule called to activity, they are useless people and therefore little understood in a world that measures everything by utility and cash value. Unlike the poet they do not return bearing artefacts, but remain in the desert, pointing to the mystery, drawing others in.

PART 1

ASPECTS OF SOLITUDE

CHAPTER 1

Society and solitude

People encounter solitude in many different ways. Some
see it as loneliness, which has been described as the charac-
teristically modern experience. But loneliness is not solitude. Loneliness, unlike solitude, is socially defined; people
experience loneliness as a lack of social worth. We live in a
society which values people largely by their usefulness to
that society; today's unemployed feel devalued because
they have no paid employment, the only value they know.
People's value has become their economic value, their
capacity to accumulate wealth on their own behalf or on
behalf of other people. Therefore the very young, the old
and the sick have no value and become second-class
citizens.

One's image of oneself is something that has been built
up from earliest childhood. One is cast in a role of sexual
and social stereotype, imbued with the values of one's
parents' outlook and status in society. Admittedly such
roles nowadays are much more varied than they were even
in our great-grandparents' day where the medieval notion
of 'states of life' still held, where one was born into a social
role, a place on the ladder, and dressed according to its
status. Universal education and Marks and Spencer have
been part of the revolution which has finally overturned the
medieval world. Only in the Roman Catholic Church is it
still visible, where 'states of life' are still spoken of.

Feminist writers, studying the role that women have
been expected to play in our society, have shown that the
self-image of many women is entirely a social construct.
So although in the modern world we have women who are
business executives, barristers, engineers, doctors and

priests, many of them are still paralysed by residual guilt at the fact that their busy and economically successful life has meant that they are not able to give themselves fully to the only role that society has until recent times allowed a woman, that of wife and mother. Such is the burden of social conditioning. We do not feel comfortable unless we are looking at an image of ourselves reflected in the mirror of the other.

Without this mirror we are lonely and have no idea of our own value. We seek affirmation of ourselves and our role in the world. We are someone's son or daughter, someone's brother, someone's mother, someone's employee, someone's boss. Unemployment or retirement ejects us from the world of work, with its hierarchy of values and its affirmation of our competence and worth. Death or enforced separation may remove us from those we love and who love us. Deprived of our systems of self-affirmation we are lonely; we have no value to anyone.

This sort of loneliness is an affliction of modern society, and is part of what Marx called 'false consciousness', by which a person is alienated from a truly human consciousness into a system of values which, like the flickering images of the television screen, appear as real but which are an illusion. The political and religious institutions of this society are constructed to reinforce the values of such a society; they have no point of reference outside that society. Political institutions offer a strictly limited choice; the only alternative to such systems is revolution, after which society settles down to reformulate its political institutions on very similar lines to the old.

Religious institutions tend to reinforce the status quo, the divinely ordered state of society, as in England with the established Church: Church and State holding society together like a pair of bookends. There has always been this institutional element in religion, but it has been countered by the prophetic element which says firmly that truth does not lie in the accepted, the comfortable and the conformist way of life. The prophet is the outsider, the one who dwells

16

in the wilderness, with the minimum stake in society and spurning the comforts offered by it. As solitary, the prophet criticizes society in the name of a higher authority and a wider vision of what society could be.

What is the difference between loneliness and solitude? The one who is lonely is one who feels deprived of what the socially constructed vision of reality leads him or her to believe is his/her right in society. The solitary on the other hand stands alone, not seeking validation in society but in the vision of something greater beyond that society. Solitude itself provides the necessary distance from the hall of mirrors.

The solitary is not necessarily one who withdraws from society, but one who can cast a cold eye upon society's institutions. There are those who by nature are social misfits, those who have not been socialized into conformity with social norms. Their non-conformity may have pathological elements, but there are amongst them those who are the creators and originators whose very nature makes them independent of society's values. Their creative potential can often lead them into ways which ordinary people find odd. In a sense they create at the expense of what most people would regard as normal life. But without such people the greatest heights of the human spirit would never be reached. The great discoveries of art, music, literature and science would never have been made, and the technical marvels which we take for granted in today's world would never have been developed.

These innovators are those who stand outside the world which most of us come to terms with. Their eyes are fixed on the horizon beyond which lies the possibility of something new, something yet unknown. They move always into the future, into the world of becoming, which is inevitably a place of solitude inhabited by few others.

There are also those whose individual enterprise is made at the expense of society. Such are the business tycoons whose abilities are put at the service of a personal pursuit of power and the accumulation of wealth. Such men (for they are nearly always men) have existed throughout history. In times past they were often soldiers and conquerors, sweeping their way across the world in the pursuit of power and status in an orgy of destruction and disruption of ordered societies. Alexander 'the Great', after having imposed himself upon most of the known world of his time, wept because he had no more worlds to conquer. Such men are indeed solitary from choice, since all they touch is turned to ashes and their empires, whether military empires or business empires, crumble at their deaths and they leave no lasting monument or benefit to the world.

The heroes of the classical world on the other hand are solitaries of a different sort. They were men who were called upon to be carriers of a particular destiny, to be bearers of perils and suffering. They are never less than human, but are archetypes – of exile, like Odysseus, of tragic destiny, like Oedipus, of personal honour, like Achilles. Their superhuman qualities led to their cult being established and sacrifices being offered to them, rather as in later times Christian saints were raised to the altar and granted a cult with veneration. Do today's sporting heroes, with their ephemeral glory, have the same power to speak to the reaches of the human spirit?

The nineteenth century cult of heroes was a cult of leadership. Victorian heroes and heroines were those who typified a particular strength and courage, combined with a capacity for self-sacrifice, appropriate to an entrepreneurial society which emphasised success and personal achievement. Their triumph was a triumph of the will over adverse circumstances. They were self-made heroes, rather than those who in the Greek tales obeyed and fulfilled the will of the gods. Odysseus, as Homer depicts him, voyaged for no purpose that he understood, the bearer of the cosmic conflict between Zeus, the god of an ordered and stable world, and Poseidon, the god of earthquakes and of the restless and ever-changing sea.

Today's heroes have no power to enlarge our vision of life; they are merely those who perform feats that we

18

should vicariously wish to identify with. Accompanied by television cameras (whose unheroic operators do not share the credit) they climb Everest, cross the Atlantic single-handed, achieve sporting prodigies, pushing human endurance to the limit, aided by all the assistance of modern science. Beyond the limits of such heroes is the fiction of Superman, who with the aid of magical powers dissolves all obstacles and resolves all conflict. Superwoman on the other hand, we may note in passing, is merely one who successfully manages to hold together all the roles that the modern world places upon women.

The ancient heroes, like the Christian saints, are those who bear a particular burden of human suffering, illuminating the change and mutability of human life and pointing to a meaning beyond the merely human. They are bearers of meaning, of transcendence.

Making the divine a human reality is the function of the shamans of 'primitive' societies. The ecstatic trances of the shaman are voyages to another world of the spirit which gives meaning to this one. The shaman's role as spiritual guide and healer depends upon this ability to move between the two worlds, the seen and the unseen. Men or women usually become shamans following a period of affliction or sickness, which resolves itself when they submit to being channels of the spirits. As such, they are solitaries.[1]

Affliction and the bearing of burdens appear in the lives of the biblical prophets. Their spiritual burden was the word of the Lord which drove them to speak to the people who would rather not listen to such disturbing things. Amaziah the priest of Bethel tells Amos to go away and prophesy somewhere else, not at Bethel, the royal sanctuary and national temple. "I am no prophet," Amos replies, "nor a prophet's son; but I am a herdsman, and a dresser of sycamore trees, and the LORD took me from following the flock, and the LORD said to me, 'Go prophesy to my people Israel'" (Amos 7: 12-15). The pressure of the spirit was irresistible: "The lion has roared:

19

who will not fear? The Lord GOD has spoken; who can but prophesy?" (Amos 3:8).

Isaiah said, "The LORD spoke thus to me with his strong hand upon me," (Is 8:11) "and warned me not to walk in the way of this people." Solitude was thrust upon the prophets; Jeremiah complains: "I have become a laughingstock all the day, every one mocks me. For whenever I speak, I cry out, I shout, 'Violence and destruction!' For the word of the LORD has become for me a reproach and derision all day long. If I say, 'I will not mention him, or speak any more in his name,' there is in my heart as it were a burning fire shut up in my bones, and I am weary with holding it in, and I cannot" (Jer 20:7-9).

The person of the solitary holds together two worlds, the place of exile and the place from which the solitary is exiled. Reconciliation of the two may be the task; always attempted but never achieved. The solitary is the voice crying in the wilderness; the cry is one of necessity, the burden which is imposed, whether or not the cry is heard. The prophets were possessed by a blinding vision of God's truth and justice which demanded acknowledgement.

A sense of separation marked the earliest Christian communities, which had begun as a Jewish sect and had in time separated into a distinct body. The earliest Christians had attended the temple and synagogue regularly, but they were eventually expelled and formed their own places of worship. They saw themselves as the new Israel, the righteous remnant who were faithful to God's commands. The entry to the new community was by baptism, not circumcision which was the mark of the old Israel. Just as circumcision set apart Israel, so baptism or washing set apart the Christians, and this difference was marked in their behaviour. The Epistle to Diognetus, which dates probably from the second century has this to say about Christians: "Though they live at home in their own countries, they behave more like those who live in a transit camp. They take their share in all things as citizens, but they also submit to hardships as if they were aliens. For them, every foreign country is a homeland, and a homeland a foreign country."[2]

This sense of separation became more marked under the violent persecutions that were launched from time to time by the Roman authorities. In the eyes of those authorities the refusal of Christians to offer sacrifice to the emperor marked them as impious, the enemies of the Roman state. As such they had to be eliminated with the barbaric cruelty typical of the ancient world. Persecution continued, fluctuating in violence, until religious toleration was proclaimed with the so-called Edict of Milan in 313. Following this, and the favour shown by the emperor Constantine to the Christians, Christianity became fashionable and instead of being the difficult and separate way followed by the few it was embraced by all. Baptism lost its significance as a mark of separation, and martyrdom, the identification with the death of Christ, was no longer the crown of the Christian life.

For those who had staked their lives on their separateness, this was an intolerable state of affairs, though for some it must have provided welcome relief. Martyrdom, the way of suffering, had been the focus of the Christian life for so long. Ignatius of Antioch, as he travelled towards a martyr's death in the Colosseum in Rome, had identified that death with the offering of the Christian Eucharist: "I am God's wheat, and I am ground by the teeth of wild beasts that I may be found pure bread (of Christ)."[3] Now sacrifice had to be expressed in some other way. Gradually there began the flight to the desert. Men and women sought the lonely and uncultivated places beyond human settlement where they could pursue in solitude the life of affliction and hardship which persecution had until now provided. This became known as the white martyrdom which took the place of the martyrdom of blood. It was a life of prophetic separation from the way of life current in the Roman world. To this movement we shall return later.

The classical world, unaffected by the Hebrew and Christian tradition of a God who entered into a dialogue with humanity, had a different view of solitude. Solitude was the milieu of the philosopher and the contemplation of the Good, the True and the Beautiful, the eternal verities. The philosopher dwelt in *otium*, idleness, unconcerned with the practical life. The arts of poetry and music were admitted, but not arts such as painting or sculpture which involved the work of the hands. This denigration of manual labour has had lasting influence in Western civilization, even in the monastic world where manual labour was an essential part of the original monastic vocation. The separation of the philosopher was therefore the separation from practical life into the realm of the mind, or intellect. The idea of contemplation as being primarily an intellectual or mental process entered Christian thinking through writers trained in the classically formed schools, not always with helpful results. Fortunately it has been balanced by the ancient wisdom tradition of monasticism, with its emphasis on *praxis*. But it is difficult not to see that the traditions of the ancient world, where civilized life was based on a large under-class of slaves, lay behind the later growth of lay brothers in the monastery who did the work while the choir monks gave themselves to the *opus dei*, or work of contemplation.

The concept of philosophical detachment has nevertheless a prophetic value. The role of the intellectual, the descendant of Plato's philosopher, has been examined by Edward Said in his Reith Lectures 1993. Despite the intellectual's involvement in all aspects of modern living and his/her enlistment in the service of various ideologies and techniques of persuasion, the intellectual stands as a person capable of a solitary viewpoint, a point of freedom and detachment.

Today's intellectual cannot dwell in *otium*, but has to subject the stereotypes, the modern idols, to dissection and analysis. The perception of the truth, and the proclaiming of it in the face of all pressures to the contrary and in rejection of all rewarding temptations to speak differently, is the fruit of the intellectual's detachment and solitude. It is a struggle akin to that of the monks of the desert, as they fought with illusory demons and temptations to find purity of heart. Like the monk's, the temptations of the intellectual come from within his/her own mind as well as from without in the shape of those who seek to recruit the intellectual in the service of their particular illusion.

Although it is the task of the intellectual to enter into dialogue with the world of politics and ideas, this has to be done from a place of detachment outside the systems. The creative intellectual, as apart from the journeyman whose methods are pragmatic ones, is the one capable of new insights and methods of thinking. This capacity is born in solitude and detachment, the fruit of original thought in dialogue with existing problems and ideas but with the ability to perceive everything with fresh eyes, and to find new points of entry into old problems as well as discovering new fields to explore.

The solitary then, although separated in a greater or lesser degree from everyday human society, is a point of reference for that society. The very existence of the solitary as one who stands outside the systems of values and rewards with which society supports and drives itself, calls into question these systems and as such enables people to free themselves from them. One can be solitary within the system by freely choosing a different philosophy to live by and by rejecting the values and rewards such a system offers. Such a path is essentially solitary as it finds no foothold in the places most people live in, either from necessity or choice, or because they have never experienced essential solitude or achieved the capability for detached observation. Such a solitary existence questions society's values and points to a human authenticity as a point of reference by which society and its institutions may be judged.

NOTES

1. I.M. Lewis, *Ecstatic Religion*, Penguin Books 1971.
2. *Epistle to Diognetus*, V. 5.
3. Ignatius of Antioch, *Epistle of Ignatius to the Romans*, 4.

CHAPTER 2

The artist as solitary

A solitary existence is the lot of the creative artist, whether in the field of music, poetry or the visual arts. The Greek word *poietes*, from which our word poet derives, means maker, and the work of the artist is essentially that of creating artefacts. These artefacts are the verbal, visual or aural equivalent of the world in which we live, the original creation, the given. Unlike the original creation depicted in the book of Genesis, the creation of the artist is not *ex nihilo*, from nothing, but from the materials of the already existing world. In Aristotle's view there is nothing in the mind that has not entered by means of sense-perception, which means that the furniture of our mental processes is already in place. Originality consists in the perception of new paths and the formulation of new concepts which must, even in the most abstruse realms of scientific thinking, have some relationship to what has gone before. Without some recognisable pattern they would be unintelligible to others.

The work of the artist is essentially communication, the actualising of the perceptions reached by the creative individual, the formulation of the original vision into words, sounds, shapes and colours. The wrestling with the materials produces something which is a new experience for those who hear or see the end product. Finishing the work is analogous to giving birth to a child; the completed artefact is sent forth into the world to achieve its own existence. For the artist the struggle of creation is finished: Picasso once said that when a painting was hung on a wall it was dead for him. Wordsworth on the other hand spent many years working on his long poems, delaying the final moment before the child was finally brought to book and published.

The mystery of the work of the poet, the maker, is the sharing in the divine work of the creation of the world. According to the biblical tradition the world is not a divine emanation, nor is it itself divine, but the work of God's hands (Ps 8:3,6; Ps 19:1; Ps 103:22). Human beings too are the work of God's hands:

> "...we are the clay, and you are our potter,
>   we are all the work of your hand" (Is 64:8).

This shaping and making, the bringing of order out of chaos, is an essential part of artistic creation, and is a profoundly solitary activity. Even in what would appear to be a social activity such as entertainment this is so; the late Ewan MacColl, the folk-singer, said that when singing before an audience he was profoundly alone. The inner experience cannot be shared; it is the resulting artefacts which are shared, the poems, the paintings, the music, the drama. Indeed, for music and drama performance, communication is essential for this sharing process. The composer, the dramatist, hands over his or her child as it were, for others to bring up.

The work of art is both revelation and concealment; the artist both reveals his or her inner self and constructs an alternative reality which stands in front of that inner self. The artist constructs an alternative persona, the mask which like that used in Greek drama stands in for real life. Behind the mask the human person is often disorganised and chaotic; the lives of many artists are notoriously free of social constraints and conventions. It is as if the judgments required in the day-to-day work of creation were confined to this work and did not apply behind the mask.

For James Joyce the creative process was essentially one of struggle against the accepted values of society:

25

"When we are living a normal life we are living a conventional one, following a pattern which has been laid out by other people in another generation, an objective pattern imposed on us by the church and state. But a writer must maintain a continual struggle against the objective: that is his function. The eternal qualities are the imagination and the sexual instinct, and the formal life tries to suppress both."[1]

Anthony Storr makes the interesting observation that many poets suffer periods of mental instability resulting in confinement in institutions.[2] He suggests that writing poetry is an attempt to bring order out of chaos, and that the poetry springs from the poet's struggle with reality. The therapist of course may have a different concept of reality from the poet. It could be that poetry springs from a deeper layer of chaos in the personality, the primal chaos from which the world was created, and that the poet is more familiar with it. The 'making' of the poet is the giving of form and shape to that which comes to birth from that primal chaos. The poet is Daedalus, the marvellous artificer, whose name James Joyce used for his hero. Daedalus constructed the labyrinth at Knossos in which the Minotaur was kept, the primal monster who devoured human victims. It was Daedalus who invented the art of flying, moving above the earth into the heavenly sphere, the image of the solitary creator.

Flying has now of course become a commonplace of modern living, a convenient form of rapid transport from place to place, a celestial omnibus. Daedalus' flying made the transition from one element to another, from Earth to Air, which meant that he had power over the elements, the basic reality-stuff which bound all others. Air was the place of the soul, breathed into the body. Daedalus, by his cunning skill, makes himself at home here.

For Aristotle the soul was borne upon the winds and enters the body from the universe by respiration.[3] For the Greeks, as for the Hebrew prophets, divine inspiration was breathed into the body from outside. Inspiration is a term still used in connection with the artistic process, an expression of the experience that artistic creation is something which is given from outside, a process which carries the artist along in the grip of something which directs the work, and of which one is but the instrument.

Alexander Goehr, Professor of Music at Cambridge University, has given a brilliant account of the process of writing music, which anyone engaged in artistic creation of whatever sort will recognise. The journey begins, he says, with:

> "...personal, subjective, sensual imaginings, which are commonly grouped together under the general heading of inspiration, to an almost impersonal trance-like state, in which the act of creation takes place; and finally – but alas, not inevitably – to an ascent to a state of bliss, a condition of mysterious marriage in which the self no longer acts as a self but seems momentarily at one with the material of its contemplation."

The early stages of creative activity are, he says, characterised by intentions and vague fantasies of musical textures and forms. False starts are made, intentions are not realised. Nothing seems to progress:

> "In total gloom I sit and contemplate the shards of my vanity. Because I know now that the inspiration, the idea which seemed so promising only a moment ago, is as dust and no more than an attempt to short-circuit the necessary progress whereby I free myself from myself, as the poet Stefan George wrote, 'to breathe the air of other planets'. This is a time of almost total darkness, in which those around me seem clumsy and hostile; a time when I am oppressed by the disorder that surrounds me."

This is the place of primal chaos, of deconstruction or decomposition, the descent into Avernus which Dante travelled in the 'Inferno', the compulsive journey which must be undertaken before the ascent to paradise is attained. This journey, Goehr says,

"is the essential if painful path out of the prison of the self – a necessary stage, perhaps even the price to be paid for what is to come. For it seems to me at the nadir, the moment of total blackness, when 'the sun shall be darkened, and the moon shall not give her light and the stars of heaven shall fade...then shall I see.' Then I make the signs (few in number) on the blank paper, and these notes, this apparently involuntary and unintentional act, this letting go of the archer's bowstring without even taking any aim, releases an arrow. It releases me from the prison of my impotence, so that together, the arrow and I, fly I know not where."

He continues:

"...the music writes itself: the identification with the material – the notes, the rhythms and their implied continuations – is complete. There is no longer a composer who pushes the material about, but only its servant, carrying out what the notes themselves imply. This is the exact experience I seek and which justifies all else..."[4]

Although the creation of the poet is a creation at second remove from the first, the pit of darkness, the Avernus, which the poet must enter, places the original creation in the cauldron, the melting-pot. Cauldrons are a great feature of Celtic mythology; Bran's Cauldron of Renovation brought the dead back to life. Taliesin, in the Welsh tale, obtains his poetic and prophetic gifts by accident, from the cauldron of Inspiration and Science which the hag Ceridwen set to boil for a year and a day, and which had been placed in his charge. Three drops of the liquor flew out of the cauldron on to his finger, which he immediately placed in his mouth.

28

In the creative process, the artist is essentially solitary, not following any paths made by the feet of others. This freedom results in the perception of new patterns or new interpretation of data, the recombination of words or sounds, shapes or colours to produce the new experience which any work of art is. In this solitary work of creation the artist plays God. "What a great work you have done for God!" exclaimed a nun to Matisse, when he had completed his paintings in the Chapel of the Rosary at Vence. "I did it for myself," said Matisse. "But you told me you were doing it for God," said the nun. "Yes," insisted Matisse, "but I am God".

The artist is in a sense a counter-creator, the Prometheus who stole the divine fire and who created men out of clay. The price of the artist's presumption is suffering. Prometheus was bound upon a rock, where an eagle perpetually tore at his liver. Daedalus' son Icarus, who was equipped with wings by his father, came unstuck when he flew too near the sun. Orpheus himself, who entered the underworld to bring back his beloved Eurydice and charmed the spirits there by his playing, finally lost her when he disobeyed instructions and turned his head. There are limits to sacred power given to humans. Yet it is the exploration of these boundaries which provides the greatest art, and it is both a tragic and a solitary experience.

What is solitude? Essentially, it is separation, most obviously from the company of others, but also from the labels which are tied on to things, labels which name, define and price the values of society, the way it sees things. The labels become a substitute for the things themselves. Artistic creation is a journey into freedom, essentially a matter of making something new, of finding a new language, a new vision.

For Wordsworth, the purpose of his solitary expeditions was the exploration of a whole new world of inward experience. Poetry was no longer to be written after classical models but to be spun from the raw materials of everyday experience. What he sought was not just a romantic

29

vision of Nature but an exploration into his own solitude, a new sensibility where the springs of poetic imagination were fed from a new and deeper source: "that inward eye which is the bliss of solitude." His solitude involved explorations into the sources of poetry itself, not only into language but into the power of poetry to create new visions of the world:

"... Visionary power
Attends the motion of the viewless winds,
Embodied in the mystery of words:
There, darkness makes abode, and all the host
Of shadowy things work endless changes, – there,
As in a mansion like their proper home,
Even forms and substances are circumfused
By that transparent veil with light divine,
And, through the turnings intricate of verse,
Present themselves as objects recognised,
In flashes, and with glory not their own."[5]

The product of the poetic imagination is not just a new vision but a new language. Wordsworth's famous statement from the preface to the 'Lyrical Ballads', which he and Coleridge published in 1798, "Poetry is the spontaneous overflow of powerful feelings: it takes its origin from emotion recollected in tranquillity" is a statement about the springs of poetry, not about the work of making which went on in the solitude or tranquillity of the poet's study, or (according to Dorothy Wordsworth) while walking up and down in the rain, alone under an umbrella. In classical terms, inspiration, or possession by the divine spirit (*pneuma*) was regarded as necessarily being accompanied by intense stimulation of the emotions, so Wordsworth was here placing his work in a classical context.

Wordsworth's 'viewless winds' was a phrase borrowed from Shakespeare; from Claudio's meditation on death in 'Measure for Measure', III.i.116:

"Ay, but to die, and go we know not where;
To lie in cold obstruction and to rot;
This sensible warm motion to become
A kneaded clod; and the delighted spirit
To bathe in fiery floods, or to reside
In thrilling region of thick-ribbed ice;
To be imprisoned in the viewless winds,
And blown with violence round about
The pendent world!"

A phrase furnished with many echoes of descent into darkness, turning stairs, winding sheets. The poet's vision emerges from this dark world of shadows, and through the medium of language the world is reborn as something which is recognised but transformed with a divine light.

The power of the artist to present a new vision of the world is the fruit of inward solitude and detachment from the everyday world which would seek to translate and diminish creative power into its own service. The artist must step aside into a prophetic solitude which demands a total allegiance. Without this prophetic solitude art becomes a bourgeois or academic exercise which is merely the reflection of the values of society, a sort of mirror where society can smugly regard its own image. Bourgeois art has no vision of anything beyond its immediate horizons; Warhol's tin of Campbell's soup is reality. This is an art which denies solitude, and says that what art is all about is a trick of vision, the way you look at reality.

The artists of the Dada period (also in many ways a bourgeois movement) opened windows into the strangeness and ambiguity of experience, at much the same time as Sigmund Freud was exploring the unknown recesses of the unconscious mind. But their successors today would seem to be denying that there is any artistic experience at all beyond that of a certain technical skill. Even technical mastery would seem to be discounted. Today's anti-art refuses the journey into solitude. The observer and the observed are one; the picture does not point beyond the merely visual experience except in the form of jokes or visual ambiguities. This attempt at a value-free art, an art of exclamation, removes from art all human experience. It is, like all bourgeois art, an art without suffering.

Prophetic art, born of solitude, is revolutionary art, not in the sense of being tied to a particular ideology but by being the art of the frontier, across which raids are made into previously unexplored territory. The artist's experience of solitude is transformed in wrestling with words, paint, patterns of sound, into a new experience which is offered to those who remain on the near side of the frontier. The work of the artist is the creative work of bringing form out of the primal chaos.

The poet returns from his solitude, bearing gifts. But the country of solitude which we shall presently explore has many more resources than the quarries and springs of artistic achievement. It is a hidden country, known only to those who travel in it. Beyond every mountain range there lies another. From this land we return bearing no artefacts and few words.

NOTES

1. James Joyce, recorded by Arthur Power. Quoted in John Bishop, *Joyce's Book of the Dark*, pp 423-4. University of Wisconsin Press 1986.
2. Anthony Storr, *Solitude*, Fontana Paperbacks 1989.
3. Aristotle, *On the Soul*.
4. Alexander Goehr, article in 'The Independent', 11 May 1991, reprinted by kind permission of the author.
5. Wordsworth, *The Prelude*, Book 5, line 595.

CHAPTER 3

Physical solitude

There was once a little boy who lived on a remote hill farm in Wales. One day he rushed in to his mother in great excitement, "Our mam, our mam, I saw a man on the mountain. And I saw another man on the mountain last week. What a lot of people there are in the world, our mam!" Such physical solitude is possible today only in a few places in the world. Even when I was told the story, many years ago, it was a memory of the past, a lost Eden. The solitary life of the hill-shepherds has all but gone, regretted by some but not by others, together with the poetic and religious inspiration that often went with it.

Physical solitude, however fleeting, still has power over us. We are cast upon our own resources in such solitude, which holds boundless possibilities as well as a vaguely obscure threat to all that we live by. Such experiences provide a sense of distance from the familiar, a stepping outside of everyday relationships. Those who live with this sense of distance are aware of living within boundaries and what the boundaries are. To live on the frontier involves us in living with the reality of two worlds.

"God made the country, and man made the town," wrote the poet Cowper,[1] trying to express the sense of distance. Not literally true of course, since the British country landscape is man-made too, and very different from the primeval forest which once covered the land. Most seekers after solitude do in fact seek rural seclusion, to match the physical isolation to the sense of separation from the received values of society. Yet there are hermits in the cities too, who find their solitude in the isolation and loneliness of city life.

Country solitude, for those escaping from the city, is inevitably coloured by the poetry of Wordsworth, a country-dweller, and by the ideas of the Romantic Movement of the early nineteenth century. Even the green movements of today are influenced by dreams of a primal, innocent Eden. The self-sufficiency movement of the sixties was an attempt at creating an ideal world far removed, not only from the city, but also from the reality of the subsistence farming which had been carried on for hundreds of years in the very places where they chose to realise their green dreams.

The pastoral idyll from classical times, from Horace's Sabine farm to Marie Antoinette's playing at milkmaids in the Petit Trianon, opposes country to city as representing freedom from collective responsibility, social and sexual. Arcadia, inhabited by shepherds and huntsmen, was a dream-world in these fantasies. The pastoral has a long literary history from Theocritus to Virgil to Sir Philip Sidney's 'Arcadia' and Shakespeare's 'As You Like It'. (As Raymond Williams wryly points out, it is not easy to forget that Sidney's Arcadia, which gives a continuing title to English neo-pastoral, was written in a park which had been made by enclosing a whole village and evicting the inhabitants.[2]) In 'La Traviata' Violetta and Alfredo retire to the country for their idyll of love, until the money runs out.

Solitude, as the Romantic Movement thought about it, was a delicious contrast to the busy world of affairs and expanding trade. The paintings and engravings of the period show us empty landscapes, peopled by a few shepherds with their sheep or by a hermit in his cell beneath towering and inaccessible crags. Unlike the landscapes of the previous century which are serene classical idylls, these landscapes are an exploration of the beauties of nature, an exercise in sensibility, a setting for sublime feelings. Perspectives are exaggerated, the effects of light and shade are used to dramatize the scene.

Ironically, the Romantic Movement arose at a particular period in history, when the beautiful river-valleys of England and Wales were being despoiled in the search for power-sources to run the mills and foundries of the Industrial Revolution. When Wordsworth wrote of the 'sylvan Wye' in his 'Lines written a few miles above Tintern Abbey' he ignores the fact that the Wye valley near Tintern was in fact an industrial site, with commercial traffic on the river and iron-furnaces along its banks, whose smoke, Gilpin noted in his *Observations on the River Wye* (1792) "issuing from the sides of the hills; and spreading a thin veil over part of them, beautifully breaks their lines, and unites them with the sky".[3] Even industry could be Romantic.

The industry has departed from Tintern today, although in the tourist season the rush of coaches through the Wye Valley brings pollution of a different kind. Many of the 'beauty-spots' visited by today's tourists, the Romantics of the twentieth century, bear hidden traces of their industrial past. Nature has recovered the beauty: the solitude, alas, has departed.

In this period too, gardening reflected the view of nature as solitude into which one entered for re-creation. Today's view of the countryside as a place of leisure and recreation, essentially an urban view, is a descendant of this standpoint. Early ideas of gardening meant the enclosure of a space; the garden was a place set aside for the cultivation of fruit, herbs and delicate vegetables. With the introduction of roses and other flowers it also became a pleasure-garden where one could enjoy idleness. In Islamic cultures the garden became a place of paradise where one could escape from the heat and dust amongst cool marble and flowing water.

The Romantics removed this sense of enclosure, of the garden being taken out of the wilderness, by bringing the wilderness back into the garden, suitably controlled of course by the demands of fashionable sensibility. Walls were levelled, to be replaced by the ha-ha which gave the illusion of distance. What enclosure remained was arranged to present a series of experiences, focal points in the general idea of a country walk. Artificial 'hermitages' and grottoes were introduced to maintain the illusion of the experience of Nature as primal experience, as solitude.

This willed experience of solitude was a reflection upon human life, a distancing of oneself from society. At best it was a dream of original innocence, of paradise lost; at worst it was aesthetic posturing. There is no way back to Eden. The biblical view is one of progression towards a final consummation; as the Orthodox theologian P. Evdokimov puts it: "The Kingdom is not simply a return back towards paradise, but its forward-moving creative fulfilment which takes in the whole of creation."[4]

Physical solitude becomes rarer in our overpopulated world, where the countryside is seen as a leisure facility. Anyone visiting the Lake District today in spring or summer in search of Wordsworth's solitary experience would be sadly disappointed. The relentless erosion caused by countless feet destroys the tranquil beauty which people seek. Whatever they are seeking, it is not solitude. The concept of 'leisure' is itself a romantic idea, in opposition to the idea of work as unremitting toil which industrial life imposed. The 'idle rich' had leisure.

Leisure in fact is not a concept belonging to the country. A farmer's life is one especially notable for the absence of leisure, since it occupies the whole of daylight hours, in the way work did in the past before the passing of protective legislation enabling workers to enjoy leisure. The nearest thing to leisure for the farmer is market day, and much of that is taken up with buying and selling. What the countryman has enjoyed in the past, and still does even today in his work, is solitude, although the clatter of tractors and other farm machinery tends to destroy the silence which once accompanied it. The modern ploughman working in a closed tractor-cab with the radio going experiences a different solitude from that of his ancestors; perhaps it is more of an insulation from solitude than an experience of something greater than oneself of which one is part.

The capacity to be alone is an art largely forgotten in the modern world. It is an ability to live with oneself without props, without the emotional reinforcement provided by others and by accepted ideas. Solitude is a place where one dwells with a sense of distance, not a place from which one returns to reality, as one returns from a weekend in the country to our 'real' lives.

Seeking solitude is for most people an intermittent experience. Solitude is something for which they thirst but which few can find as an uninterrupted way of life. Even in our periods of solitude we are aware of our physical needs, our common humanity, which earths any temptation to regard ourselves as purely 'spiritual' beings, who live like angels between heaven and earth. Monastic tradition has always insisted upon keeping the balance between the needs of the body and the needs of the spirit. What we need is a simplification of our life, where many things we have grown to look upon as essential are treated as relative.

In our first tastes of solitude, in our country weekend, we are chiefly aware of the pleasure of being separated from our ordinary everyday existence and its pressure. 'Getting away from it all' seems such an attractive proposition; to escape from the pressures of modern life, from the telephone, from the demands of people, from the noise of urban existence. Separation from these things brings relief, and freedom. This is God's Sabbath, the seventh day of creation, where work ceases. Like God, we contemplate creation and perceive it as good.

Here we are not tourists, seeking for accepted notions of what is 'beautiful', imposing ideas which we have brought with us. This is the 'civilized' response to experience, to draw new experience into a received framework, to impose meaning upon the experience, to make it ours, part of our being-in-the-world. In solitude we are separated from our ordinary responses to become experience itself. This sometimes happens when listening to music, where one forgets one's knowledge of musical theory and history to become one with the music itself. When contemplating nature one becomes aware of oneself as part of creation, not as a separate being, but in relationship to all that is.

The ninth century Irish hermit writes of his joy in his hidden solitude:

"I wish, O son of the living God, O ancient eternal
    King,
For a hidden little hut in the wilderness that it may be
    my dwelling.
An all-grey lithe little lark to be by its side,
A clear pool to wash away sins through the grace
    of the Holy Spirit.
Quite near, a beautiful wood around it on every side,
To nurse many-voiced birds, hiding it with its shelter.
A southern aspect for warmth, a little brook across
    its floor.
A choice land with many gracious gifts such as be
    good for every plant...
Raiment and food enough for me from the King of
    fair fame,
And I be sitting for a while praying God in every
    place."[5]

What pleasures does solitude hold? The greatest perhaps is that of silence. The silence which begins as an absence of noise presses upon us. It is an exterior solitude which encompasses us, a glimpse of the desert where the stimulation of our physical senses is reduced to the minimum.

In silence and solitude we are separated from the time-scale of our usual existence. Modern life is ruled by clock-time, which imposes a rigid framework upon our nights and days. Without a clock we are returned to the time-scale of the child, the lover and the contemplative. The rhythms of the sun and moon, the rhythm of our bodies, regulate our life. These diurnal rhythms are echoed in the rhythms of the changing seasons which in an urban existence pass almost unnoticed. The mutability of nature, where things change from one substance to another, the seasons of growth, decay and death, are replaced in the city by a life of constant change, where something new is always demanded, a culture of eternal youth, where death is unspeakable.

In solitude one learns to be alone. Without the mirrors of oneself that other people provide, the ready-made roles that one habitually plays, one is faced with the depths of one's own self which do not usually find a place in one's daily life. The task is to explore these depths, to befriend them, and make them one's own. This is a journey of exploration into unknown territory that lies in the distance beyond the horizon.

There is of course darkness in these depths, which one will sooner or later encounter if one travels far enough. This was well known by the early monks and by those who followed in their footsteps. In order to travel into this underworld one needs external structures of some sort to provide a frame of reference. Like Odysseus on Calypso's isle, we have to construct a new boat to enable us to sail onwards in these treacherous seas. More will be said about this subject in later chapters.

So far we have spoken of chosen solitude, that which is freely undertaken. But for some the solitude they find is imposed upon them from without, and not of their own choosing. Defoe's Robinson Crusoe responded to being cast away upon a desert island with all the enterprise one would expect of the Protestant work ethic current in his period. The contrast between a civilised man and the world of 'nature' was a theme which was to continue to fascinate for a long time yet.

The separation of the 'civilised' man is a form of alienation from the natural world. Robinson Crusoe's fear at finding a strange footprint in the sand was the fear of the unknown, the 'savage' world beyond his control. His possession of a gun and an axe, survivals from the shipwreck in which all his companions perished, gave him control over the possibility of destruction. He sets to work to strengthen his stockade. His solitude is the place of the unknown challenge and the fight against adversity, aided by the tools of civilisation.

Coleridge's 'Ancient Mariner', significantly written in poetic form rather than as a novel, appeared some eighty years later, in 1798. Here the solitude experienced by the Mariner is not one of separation from 'civilisation' but an interior one, an inability to love either the world of nature or his fellow human beings. His destruction of the albatross, the bird of good omen which brought a fair wind, is a denial of the spirit and the possibility of transcendence.

"Instead of the cross, the Albatross
About my neck was hung."

There is a deadly calm, the sea stagnates, his companions die, and he is left alone on the ocean of desolation:

"Alone, alone, all, all alone,
Alone on a wide, wide sea!"

At length, as he is watching the water-snakes in the moonlight his arid soul is moved by their beauty and a spring of love gushes from his heart. He is suddenly able to pray, and the Albatross falls from his neck. He is now able to return home, where he is met by the pilot and a 'holy Hermit', and the ship of death sinks.

The Hermit is a familiar component of the Romantic scene and here represents the truly solitary one, rather than the one who is isolated. He is a symbol of redemption and of solitude, perhaps an aspect of the poet's detachment. The isolated one cannot love, but is imprisoned in his own hell. Only by opening his heart to love is he able to escape from it. This is the message that the Mariner must carry as he reaches land, still a wanderer but delivered from interior desolation.

The prisoner's solitude is not of his own choosing. Such solitude must be endured, survival strategies have to be engineered, exterior disciplines put in place so that time is still meaningful, so that the world outside is still the dominating force. The apparatus of terror inflicted upon political prisoners is precisely designed to destroy this world, to cast the prisoner into chaos and relativity. Those who survive enforced imprisonment are those who choose the solitude, who "going through the vale of misery use it for a well",[6] who are able to use it as a place of encounter with God.

Those who are solitary through loss, sickness or old age are prisoners of circumstance. In the unchosen desert of solitude God is present only in a sense of absence. In this emptiness, when one has reached the limit of one's own resources, one is cast upon the mercy of God. The poverty and the need are the only reality. Yet it is at the end of one's tether, at the place of total abandonment, at the heart of the cross, that God is to be found, waiting for us.

NOTES

1. William Cowper, *The Task*, bk. 1, l. 749.
2. Raymond Williams, *The Country and the City*, Chatto and Windus 1973, p. 22.
3. Quoted by Stephen Gill, *William Wordsworth, a Life*, Oxford 1989.
4. Quoted by Jürgen Moltmann, *God in Creation*, SCM Press 1985, p. 348.
5. Translated by Kuno Meyer, *Selections from Ancient Irish Poetry*, Constable 1959.
6. Psalm 84, Coverdale translation, *Book of Common Prayer*, 1662.

PART 2

HISTORICAL ROOTS

CHAPTER 4

Inner solitude

The one possessed by solitude is the monk. The word 'monk' comes from the Greek word *monos*, alone. Choosing solitude is the ultimate expression of distance from society and its values, a living out of the sense of separation felt by the first Christians. Like the prophets with their blinding vision of God, the monk is called to follow a different agenda from other people. To possess the pearl of great value, like the merchant in the Gospel (Mt 13:46), the monk gives everything. Despite centuries of development of monastic life, in all the literature the monk is still seen as 'monos'. The primary call to solitude has remained the same, beneath the outward forms it has assumed, from the early hermit life of the first monks to the later elaborations of the coenobitic, or community life.

The early Christians who went into the desert were those who felt that to seek God they had to distance themselves from a world which was not so very unlike the world we live in today, filled with violence and pleasure-seeking. By means of their physical separation from the values and distractions of contemporary society they sought to occupy themselves with God alone. Their role-models were the biblical prophets, particularly Elijah, who was fed by the ravens in the wilderness, and who lived as a solitary in a cave on Mount Carmel, and John the Baptist, 'the prince of hermits', as Richard Rolle, the fourteenth century English hermit, described him. But their lives were not defined by what they were separated from but by the mysterious emptiness of the desert which drew them, the desert which has remained a symbol of the otherness of God.

The monastic way of life appeared in India well before

the Christian era, the hermit and the sannyasi or religious mendicant being familiar figures then as now. Going apart from society to live an ascetic and disciplined life was a way of life well-established in the Jewish world. We know something about the Essenes from modern archaeological excavations, and from the writings of Philo, Pliny the Elder, and Josephus. They were an exclusive society or sect who supported themselves by working at various trades. They lived strictly and were celibate, and noted particularly for their charity towards the poor and destitute, for their condemnation of slavery, and for holding all possessions in common. At first they lived in towns and villages, but gradually withdrew into seclusion by founding a settlement on the shore of the Dead Sea. The Therapeutae, another Jewish society mentioned by Philo, lived solitary lives of prayer and study. Their chief settlement was at Lake Mareotis, near Alexandria. They lived in separate houses, near enough to afford protection, but sufficient for solitude, a pattern which recurred in the later Christian settlements which arose in the wild uncultivated places south of Alexandria and along desert edges of the valley of the Nile.

So when the first Christians went into the deserts, the first ones perhaps fleeing from the recurrent persecutions of the Roman Empire, the later ones fleeing to maintain their separateness, they built upon a way of life which already existed. The first Christian ascetics, both men and women, lived a disciplined life within their own homes. Others, dependent upon a supply of water and food, lived on the outskirts of villages; some went further into the wilderness, the uncultivated places. The desert in the Bible is portrayed as the cradle of faith, the place where Abraham and his descendants wandered, depending upon God alone. Abraham was told to leave his country, his kindred and his father's house (Gen 12), and those who went to live in desert places saw themselves as followers of Abraham, casting themselves upon the providence of God. In the ancient world a man was placed in society by the family he belonged to and the obligations to family and community flowing from this. To renounce possessions, family and the pious obligations of such a life, including marriage and the continuation of the family line, must have been seen as a revolutionary act. One was indeed leaving 'the world' to become a citizen of the 'kingdom of heaven'. This terminology is of course still used today, 'the world' being contrasted with the monastic life; the physical separation of the monk being marked by the wearing of a habit and living apart in monasteries.

Nowadays monks and nuns are thought of mainly as those who live in community. But it was not always so. In the 'Life of Antony' we are given a picture of a way of life that is essentially solitary. Antony was born in Egypt about 250, the son of prosperous Christian parents, although we are told that he never cared for learning and remained illiterate. When his parents died he was about eighteen or twenty. One day in church he heard the words of the Gospel read: "You lack one thing, go, sell what you have, and give to the poor, and you will have treasure in heaven; and come, follow me" (Mk 10:21). On hearing these words Antony immediately gave away all his possessions, and provided for his younger sister by placing her with "known and faithful virgins", an early community of nuns. Antony began living on the outskirts of his village, imitating an old man who had lived the life of a hermit for many years in the next village. He worked with his hands and spent his earnings on bread and on the poor. For fifteen years, we are told, he lived like this, during which time he visited many fellow-hermits, and "like the industrious bee, gathered honey from many sources", all of which he stored in his memory.

Then, having arranged with a friend to bring him a regular supply of bread, he went to live in a tomb, at some distance from the village. Tombs were considered to be the haunt of demons, the djinns who were a familiar part of the Egyptian scene. It has been suggested that this was an ancient painted tomb, and that the apparitions of animals who appeared to Antony were suggested by the representations of ancient gods. This may however be too literal an interpretation of what was basically a psychological struggle in Antony. We are told that he was beaten by the demons, who made such a din that at night the whole place seemed to be shaken by an earthquake. Next day his friend bringing him bread found him lying senseless on the ground, and carried him to the village church. And, we are told, his friends and relations sat around Antony as round a corpse. But about midnight, when all except his friend were asleep, he came to himself and quietly asked his friend to take him back to the tomb.

Antony continued the struggle, wracked with bodily pain, but unshaken in spirit. Eventually it seemed to him that the roof opened and a ray of light descended upon him. The demons vanished, his pain ceased. He asked the vision, "Where were you, why did you allow me to suffer such pain?" And a voice came to him, "Antony, I was here, but I waited to see your fight. Since you endured, and won the battle, I will help you always and make your name known everywhere." Antony was then about thirty-five years old.

He next went to live in a deserted fort, full of snakes and scorpions, which immediately left, as they always do in the stories of saints. Snakes and scorpions are part of the desert, the place of salvation and total dependence upon God, into which he brings the Israelites from the land of Egypt (Deut 8:15). He took with him a supply of bread, and found water inside the fort. Blocking the entrance, he stayed there by himself, supplied with bread twice a year, let down in a basket from the roof. His friends and acquaintances often spent days and nights outside, hearing the sounds of conflict within. For nearly twenty years he continued in solitude, never going out. Many of those who knew him came and camped outside, and they eventually broke down the door and asked him to come out and guide them in this way of life.

Eventually Antony found his own solitude impossible in such a crowd, and his humility compromised by the demands made upon him. He then set off to go into the upper Thebaid, where he was not known. But a voice came to him and told him to go to the inner desert. "Who will show me this trackless way?" he exclaimed. But a band of nomads appeared who were travelling that way, and after three days they came to a high mountain, at the foot of which was a spring and a few palm-trees. Here he stayed, supplied from time to time with bread by the nomads and his friends, paying for it with the baskets he wove. But to avoid troubling them he asked them for tools and some seed-corn, which he sowed and thus became completely self-sufficient. He also grew vegetables and was supplied with dates by the palm-trees. In this place, the 'Inner Mountain', he remained for the rest of his life, dying in 356, at the age of a hundred and five years. In his old age, for the last twenty years, he was accompanied by two helpers.

The life of Antony, as written by Athanasius between 356 and 362, is of course hagiography not history in the modern sense. Antony is an icon of the monastic life, a sort of template or pattern upon which many subsequent accounts have been modelled. Whether he was indeed the first hermit, the eremite or inhabitant of the *eremos* or desert, he has certainly been seen as such in tradition. Jerome, in this preface to his account of Paul, 'the first hermit', remarks of Antony that it was "not so much that he was before all others, as that it was by him their passion was awakened."

We are told by Eusebius[1] of an early desert dweller: Narcissus, bishop of Jerusalem (c. 200) who "fled from the whole body of the church, and hid himself in desert and secret places and remained there many years." The earliest Christian monastic experiment in Egypt we know of was that of Frontonius who in the reign of Antoninus Pius (138-161) went to live with seventy disciples in the Nitrian desert in Lower Egypt, south of Lake Mareotis. Nitria was the place chosen by Amun, the founder of another settlement and a younger contemporary of Antony, and like him, a Copt. The Historia Monachorum, an account written at the end of the fourth century and translated into Latin by

Rufinus, who visited there in 375, describes the cells of the monks as being widely separated, the monks living in profound silence and meeting only on Saturdays and Sundays for the *synaxis*, the vigil service of prayers and readings, which involved some of them in a journey of several miles. A later account, the Historia Lausica of Palladius, who visited Nitria in 388, describes the settlement there as consisting of five thousand monks, with their own bakeries and other amenities.

At Kellia, or the Cells, nine miles further into the desert, a similar way of life was observed; solitaries living even further apart and meeting together on Sundays. Palladius says that some six hundred monks lived there. Another eighty miles into the desert, a day and a night's journey from Nitria, lay Scetis (the modern Wadi Natrun) a place of salt-marshes, said to have been founded by Macarius, a disciple of Antony, about 330. This was a place of great austerity, where water often had to be carried many miles. All these settlements, while basically eremitical, emphasised the quality of love of neighbour. If any monk failed to appear in church for the synaxis it was assumed that he was sick or dead, and someone immediately investigated. The desert was a place above all, of hospitality, as it still is. Rufinus, writing of his journey through monastic Egypt about 375 recalls: "When we were approaching this place they were aware that foreign brothers were approaching, and at once they poured out of their cells like a swarm of bees and ran to meet us." When new entrants to the settlement arrived the monks would combine to build a cell for the new arrival; some would vacate their own cell to give to the new brother and build another for themselves. Visitors would always be offered food from each monk's meagre store, bread and salt and perhaps a little oil. Cassian, who travelled around in Egypt c. 385 studying the monastic life, speaks of a most splendid feast that he and his friend Germanus were offered of three olives apiece, preserved in brine, a basket of chick peas, of which each had five, together with two prunes and a fig.[2]

Settlements usually began by disciples gathering round particular individuals who were masters of the spiritual life, a standing that they had acquired with much labour of prayer and fasting and hard manual work. In a pre-literate society the discourse of such masters was the only instruction available, and eagerly memorised by their hearers. Much of this teaching was condensed into short sayings, which would be passed round from one community to another. Some of this collection of verbal wisdom was written down by later travellers, such as Rufinus who visited Egypt, Nitria and Pispir, Antony's Outer Mountain, in 373; John Cassian who came in 385 with his friend Germanus and stayed four years, travelling amongst the monastic settlements, a journey which was to form the basis of his Institutes and Conferences written in 420-430; and Palladius who came to Egypt and visited Alexandria, Nitria and Kellia in 388. The 'old men' were given the honoured title of 'abba', father; the women, of whom less is recorded but who led the same sort of life, were known as 'amma', mother.

The authority of these 'old men' was charismatic; their wisdom and holiness was self-evident and their life of prayer transparent, the fruit of their solitary struggles. Their disciples brought their own struggles and temptations to them and were consoled by their advice and words of wisdom. Sometimes a young monk would live in the elder's cell, acting as his servant, fetching and carrying and preparing food, and receiving training in the ways of the monk. One learnt the way of life by living it; the pioneers had learned by trial and error the evasions, the escape routes of the human heart faced with the demand of a total surrender to God. The disciples also learnt how to pray, to commit the psalms to memory by constant repetition, and much of the Bible likewise. In a society with very few books memory is finely tuned to keep such things constantly in one's mind. Not many of the early monks were educated men in the modern sense; Jerome who in his thirties spent some four or five years as a hermit in the

Syrian desert, although he took his library with him, finally returned to the world of scholarship.

Work, hard physical work, was an important part of the lives of the monks. "If any one will not work, let him not eat" (2 Thess 3:10) was the biblical precept taken to heart. They built their own dwellings of mud bricks dried in the sun; these were built either as a single cell, or with two rooms, the inner one as a place of prayer. They grew vegetables, an important part of their diet, in their gardens. During the day they plaited the reeds they had gathered and wove them into baskets or mats, which were subsequently sold in the market place of the nearest town to provide bread. The bundles of reeds provided the furniture for their cells; as they sat and worked they constantly repeated psalms. Monks also undertook the hard physical work at the time of harvest; they were probably rewarded in kind, which supplied them with grain for bread.

The diet of the early monks was mainly bread and salt, with water to drink which often had to be carried long distances. Water was also necessary for steeping the reeds to make them pliable enough to work. The bread was obtained often in yearly supplies; very different from the sort of bread we are familiar with and resembling perhaps the old ship's biscuit which also had to last for long periods. It would be softened with water before eating. In some places a little oil was allowed, and vegetables grown. The diet in fact was not very different from the peasant diet of the period which allowed for little or no meat, and consisted mainly of cereal with peas, beans, or lentils, and vegetables when available.

In all this the monk was identified with the poor man, the one who depended entirely upon God for his subsistence. Later ages tended to remove this element of manual labour from the monastic life, although St Benedict in his Rule says that "they are truly monks when they live by the labour of their hands".[3] But it was seen as discipline for the body as well as the soul. Monks were to be *autarches en paso*, masters of themselves in all things, and independent of all others "in the labour of their hands, in their food, and in their clothing". This essential detachment from dependence upon other people led to dependence upon God alone. Abba Pambo, when he was dying, said to the old men standing around him, "From the time I came to this place of solitude and built my cell and lived in it, I do not remember having eaten bread which I did not earn with my own hands, nor do I regret a word which has passed my lips until the present time. Yet I go to the Lord as one who has not yet made a beginning of serving God."[4]

The dress of the monk was the normal peasant dress of the time, consisting of a short-sleeved linen tunic, with a girdle or cord to draw the tunic up out of the way during work, a short cape, and a sheepskin, used as a cloak or covering for cold desert nights. Some groups of monks also wore a small hood, but this did not resemble the later monastic cowl.[5] There was to be no show of special virtue, such as dressing in sackcloth; everything was to be simple and practical, a working man's garments. It was only later that the idea of a special monastic dress came in, the 'habit'. This then became a sign of a particular class of those dedicated to the ascetic life; the habit was bestowed upon a new arrival when he had persevered for some time. It was a sign that he was accepted by the existing monks as one of them.

NOTES

1. Eusebius, *Hist. Eccl.*, VI. 9.
2. Cassian, *Conferences*, VIII. 1
3. *Rule of St Benedict*, 48. Translation of Abbot Hunter Blair.
4. Rosweyde, *Vitae Patrum*, V. i. 16.
5. Cassian, *Institutes*, I. 1-7.

CHAPTER 5

The monastic path

The early monks struggled for 'purity of heart', the state of blessedness where one could see God (Mt 5:8). To reach this state, where God alone was the object of desire, they struggled with their human passions, the strong natural instincts for survival embodied in the desires for food and sex. Mastering their instinctive drives was the object of their ascesis, a word used originally for the training of athletes. The apostle Paul uses the athletic metaphor for the Christian life: "Every athlete exercises self-control in all things. They do it to receive a perishable wreath, but we an imperishable" (1 Cor 9:25-27).

Fasting was an important part of monastic ascesis; many of the desert monks would fast all day, eating only at nightfall. As a penitential discipline fasting, both public and private, occurs in the Bible. Fasting as a public practice is the acknowledgement of a claim, the demands made by God, Allah, the Holy One upon the people. The biblical ascetics, such as John the Baptist, led a life of continual fasting and restricted diet. Today, in the West, fasting has become a less usual practice; only amongst the Muslim communities of our cities can we see fasting carried out with its primitive rigour. As the practice of fasting as a religious observance has declined in western society, so it has returned in secular guise in the form of dieting, as a corrective to the over-indulgence in food so prevalent in the rich nations of the world, that indulgence so castigated by the desert abbas as gluttony. In recent times too we have seen a secular return to the idea of celibacy, seen as no sex as opposed to safe sex. Not quite perhaps celibacy as the desert monks would have seen it, but a counter-cultural phenomenon.

Cassian, who had travelled to Egypt in 385 from his monastery in Syria, observed that in the monasteries of Egypt the daily fast was always broken upon the arrival of a visitor. On asking with some surprise why this was so he was answered: "The opportunity for fasting is always with me... in receiving you I receive Christ; it is to him that I owe a duty of refreshment. When you have gone I shall be able to balance the hospitality offered for his sake by a stricter fast on my own account. The children of the bride-groom cannot fast while the bridegroom is with them (Mt 9:15), but when he has departed, then they will fast".[1] So in the desert charity always takes precedence over rule, as we see in the story of a brother who came to see a certain hermit. As he was leaving he said, "Forgive me, abba, for preventing you from keeping your rule." The hermit replied, "My rule is to welcome you with hospitality and to send you away in peace".[2]

The aim of the monk was to proceed from the struggle with the appetites of the body to the contemplation of divine things. This involved the redirection of the personality to a different end from the merely instinctual gratification sought by all. Not only must bodily habits be disciplined, but the whole mind-set must be changed. The tools in this ascetic struggle were, in addition to fasting, "vigils [reduction of the desire of the body for sleep]; reading, [mainly of the scriptures, for those who could read]; and "frequent compunction of the heart for remembered failures and deceptions... and so by the copiousness of our tears and the weeping of our heart we shall succeed in extinguishing the fiery furnace of our body".[3]

But this was only the first degree of self-discipline. There was also a further battle: "And let us not believe that an external fast from visible food alone can possibly be sufficient for perfection of heart and purity of body unless with it there has also been united a fast of the soul. For the soul also has its harmful foods, slander, anger, envy, *kenodoxia* (vainglory)."[4]

What is under attack here is the inner centre of the

personality, the self-regard which would raise the demands, not only the demands of the body, but the demands of the self-image to the first place in one's attention. The vainglory which sees oneself as being better or holier than others, the denigration of other people or envy of them, anger at what one sees as unjust treatment of oneself, are all symptoms of a sickness of soul, of the secret area which one has not yet surrendered to God.

This surrendering of the whole self is the key to the monastic ascesis, which, seen from an outside and perhaps hostile viewpoint may seem morbid or perverse. The natural instinct of self-preservation leads one to place one's own interests at the centre; the aim of the monk is to place God at the centre. This involves a radical dispossession, a separation from the way of life as self-interest previously followed. Later Roman ages adopted the tonsure, the mark of the Roman slave, as a sign that one was not one's own master, but God's possession.

The importance placed upon the surrender of one's own interests is the reason for the emphasis upon *diakrisis*, or discernment. The young monk, the beginner, was encouraged to consult with the 'old men', those who after many years of striving had achieved, by long experience of their own struggle, the wisdom and insight to read hearts. Discernment was a spiritual gift which enabled them to discern the areas of the personality which had not yet been surrendered. The monk's temptations were revealed, a guide to those areas which needed further working upon; Antony said, "It is an enormous human task for each of us to take responsibility for our own faults in the sight of the Lord, and to expect temptation until our dying day".[5] It was said of Amma Sarah, one of the great women of the desert, that she struggled for thirteen years against sexual temptation, but she never prayed to be released from this battle, but kept on saying: "Lord, give me strength".[6]

Not unnaturally, sexual temptations loom large in the stories from the desert, as an area of great difficulty. Nocturnal illusions were the work of demons, the spirits of contradiction who attacked with constant and persistent force the body and mind of the monk. The belief in demons or djinns was common in Egypt and still persists in the Middle East. They were masters of fantasy and imagination, mirages of the desert. The work of the monk was, by constant struggle, a purification not only of bodily appetites but of the mind from illusion.

There were failures of course, as in any human enterprise. But such was the attraction of the desert that there are many stories of men who returned to the city in despair of never conquering their appetites, but who were irresistibly drawn back to try again. The purpose of the training of athletes is to produce a perfect physical balance, which enables the body to respond without strain to the demands placed upon it. So we see in the portraits of the old abbas a perfectly balanced person, one who is unmoved by passion but one who knows all the depths and deceptions of the human heart, and with this knowledge is enabled to act with perfect charity towards others. This knowledge has not been easily obtained, but is the gold which has been purified in the furnace.

This purification is for Antony the self-emptying which will be filled with the Spirit: "And I think that when the whole body is purified, and has received the fulness of the Spirit, it has received some portion of that spiritual body which it is to assume in the resurrection of the just".[7]

Such was the attraction of the desert at this time that large numbers flocked there. Areas like Nitria, which became highly organised settlements, with a regular supply of food, together with arrangements for marketing the handwork of the monks were a long way from the simple pioneering of an Antony. Rather than the lone figure of the solitary ascetic we have a picture of an alternative community, self-sufficient and confident in their established way of life. Even the settlements at Kellia and Scetis became crowded. There were monks on the fringes of the desert all up the Nile valley, in the Sinai peninsula and into Palestine and Syria. Their fame spread by means of the accounts of travellers, the tourists of the fourth century who brought back stories of the famous abbas and their way of living. This rash of sightseers became such a nuisance that one noted abba instructed his disciple to sort out the visitors. If they were introduced by the words "Here are brothers from Jerusalem" the abba would know that they were serious seekers. If however they were brought in with the words "Here are brothers from Egypt" they would be offered a little food before being sent on their way.[8]

Already we can see a change of emphasis in the stories; from the imitation of Abraham who left everything to the Abraham to whom it was promised that he should be the father of a great nation (Gen 46:3). There are the stories of monks like Apollo and Or, from the Thebaid. Of Or it was said that he lived for many years as a solitary, before returning in his old age to the nearer desert to minister to others. Apollo first went into the desert at the age of fifteen. He returned when he was fifty-five, and drew disciples to him, finally at the age of eighty setting up a community (384/8). It is said that they lived a common life, eating at the same table.[9] Solitaries would eat alone, except for a little food taken with visitors for hospitality's sake, lest their ascesis of fasting be perceived by others.

The picture moves here from the portrait of the ascetic as solitary hero to emphasis upon a teaching role, and from spiritual parenthood to the image of fatherhood in the mould of the *paterfamilias*, the head of the household. Solitude is sought not for its own sake as a place of union with God, but as a place of training for the service of humankind. Little by little the monastic life became, instead of a sharing of the life of the poor, a sign of status, something that would become more pronounced in medieval times.

This regard for status was reinforced by the introduction of deacons and priests into the monastic settlements. The early monks found the clerical and hierarchical state irrelevant to the monastic life. The institution of churches was essentially an urban proceeding, springing from the local gathered community. The monks sought God in solitude; community was a distraction from this, even a temptation. But as the monastic settlements became more crowded, churches were introduced together with the custom of meeting on Saturday and Sunday for vigils with prayers and readings. The clergy had a social status, an element unknown in the early days when temptations against humility were to be vigorously resisted. "Fly bishops and women" was an early warning against temptation in several directions.

Most monastic settlements consisted of the characteristic pattern of groups of separate huts. Abba Apollo's community cannot have been the only one set up as a solution to the problem of many young learners seeking to live the monastic life with insufficient guidance. With so many seekers the teachers must have been thinly spread, the old one-to-one method of ascetical training not coping with the demand. The coenobitic, or common life was to become the most popular form of monastic life. The coenobium is not a community in the modern sense; although the life is lived in common this is seen as an ascetic tool in the life of the monk, where the faults of the individual will become apparent in dealing with others and will become a subject for ascetic striving. The coenobitic monk is still *monos*, solitary. The common enterprise is held together by the common Rule, the various collections of rules and precepts to which all must be totally obedient.

Pachomius is the one usually credited with the initiation of the coenobitic life. Like Antony, he was a Copt, and was born in about 292, some forty years after Antony, and died in 346, some ten years before him. His parents were pagan, so he was not brought up as a Christian. At the age of twenty he was conscripted into the Roman army and taken to the city of Thebes, where the conscripts were closely confined. In the evening some citizens brought food to the hungry conscripts, and cheered them up. Pachomius wondered who these people were, that they were so good to men they did not know, and was told that they were Christians.

The next morning the conscripts were put on a boat and taken to Antinoë. Here undoubtedly they were subjected to the ancient equivalent of square-bashing, training in Roman army discipline and methods. After the conscripts had spent some time in this training a military victory meant that they were no longer needed and they returned with joy to their villages. But Pachomius did not return home; he travelled south and went to live in a deserted temple near a Christian village where he grew vegetables and harvested dates to support himself. It is said that many people came to live there because of him and his warm sympathy for their problems. While he was there, after some time under instruction as a catechumen, he was baptized, probably at Easter as the custom was. After about three years he heard about a hermit called Palamon not far away, and he went to him and asked to be trained as a monk. After some seven years with Palamon he was gathering reeds on the river bank some ten miles to the south, when he came to a deserted village called Tabennisi, where there was a ruined temple of Isis. He heard a voice telling him that this was the place for him to build a monastery.

The situation of Tabennisi on the banks of the Nile meant that his experiment soon became known, rather as if he had built it on a main road, such as the river was, than in a place far removed as others did. It was in a fertile rather than a desert area. Soon large numbers of men flocked to join him, and Pachomius organised them according to a Roman army system that he must have been familiar with. They were arranged in different houses, each with its own governance by hand-picked men. The success of Roman armies was founded upon their genius for organisation, and such organisation would certainly be needed for the numbers that flocked to the Pachomian monasteries. According to Jerome, in his preface to his translation of the Pachomian rule, they had in each monastery "fathers and stewards, ministers, and a master of each house. A house has, more or less, forty brothers who obey the master and, according to the number of brothers, there are thirty or forty houses in

60

one monastery, and three or four houses are federated into a tribe".[10] Brothers were grouped according to the craft they practised, the shoemakers together, linen-weavers together and so forth, each under their own master. We seem to have here a precursor of the highly organised production lines which are a feature of today's industrial practice. Such a work community was probably not seen again until the experiments of Robert Owen in the early nineteenth century, at New Lanark in Scotland and at New Harmony in America.

The work was undertaken for its own sake, not merely for the occupation of the body. Even at the *synaxis*, the nightly meeting for psalms and readings, where Pachomius himself would expound the scriptures, each monk would be supplied with soaked reeds for plaiting into ropes which would later be made into baskets. The more senior the monk, the more he was expected to accomplish. Seniority was in order of entry into the monastery, and the order never changed.

Such a highly organised community had its structures of authority clearly laid down, much in the way that the Roman army had its chains of command. Rules were drawn up to regulate many areas of the life, a precedent for the many later monastic Rules, of which the Rule of St Benedict is probably the most widely known. Before his death in 346 Pachomius had established nine monasteries of men and one of women; these were known under the collective title of *koinonia*, the precursor of the medieval religious Order. The model for such communities was the early Christian community described in Acts 2:44: "All who believed were together and had all things in common."

The separation of such communities was the separation to a particular way of life, rather than the separation from all community of the Antonian monks. Obviously it was a less demanding way of life than the extreme asceticism of the desert monks; guidance was always available from those appointed to give it and from Pachomius himself who was an intensely charismatic man. The life of the Pachomian monastery must have been not so very unlike that of Egyptian village life, with the same expectation of mutual support that appears in the story of Antony where his trials and status of holy man were supported by a host of anxious fellow villagers. Antony finally succeeded in breaking this family bond by retreating to the Inner Mountain, achieving rootlessness at last. Later solitaries took up a wandering life style in order to avoid this dependency.

The monastic life as it took shape in Egypt was the pattern for all later forms of monasticism. The eremitic, the semi-eremitic and the coenobitic way are still to be found in the Eastern churches. St Basil (c. 330-379) is credited with the introduction of the monastic life into Asia Minor and eastern Europe. After education in the best pagan and Christian culture of the day at Constantinople and Athens, he made a long tour of Egypt, Syria and Mesopotamia to gain first-hand knowledge of the lives of the solitaries. He became a hermit on his own estates near Caesarea in Cappadocia, on the shores of the Black Sea. Despite this experience, or perhaps because of his knowledge of the perils of the solitary life, he became a champion of coenobitism. Despite Basil's influence through his Rule, comparable with that of Benedict in the West, the eremitic life still flourished in the eastern churches. After the fifth century the existence of eremitic and coenobitic forms of life side by side is the most notable form of eastern monasticism; in Mount Sinai, Constantinople and at Jerusalem there were monasteries of coenobites existing side by side with hermits living in complete solitude, recluses as well as those living in lauras or groups of solitaries. They all devoted themselves to prayer and manual work, and were united under a common superior.

In Palestine most of the great lauras, or semi-eremitical settlements, were situated in the mountains east of Jerusalem, towards the Dead Sea. Here the way of life was much as it had been in the Egyptian desert, in Nitria and Scetis. Each laura had a superior or spiritual father who visited each hermit two or three times a week to give him spiritual counsel and advice. The hermits met together in church on Saturdays and Sundays as they did in Egypt. The manual work also consisted largely in making baskets. These lauras were largely supplanted by coenobitic forms of monasticism by the seventh century. But the old eremitic forms are still to be found in a few places, notably Mount Athos.

NOTES

1. Cassian, *Institutes*, V. 24.
2. *Vitae Patrum*, V. xiii. 7.
3. Cassian, *Institutes*, V. 14.
4. *Ibid.*, V. 21.
5. *Vitae Patrum*, V. xv. 2.
6. *Ibid.*, V. v. 10.
7. *Letters of St Antony the Great*, tr. Derwas J. Chitty, SLG Press, Fairacres, Oxford, Letter 1.
8. *Vitae Patrum,* VIII. 26.
9. *The Lives of the Desert Fathers* (Historia Monachorum), tr. Norman Russell, Mowbray, 1980.
10. A. Veilleux, *Pachomian Koinonia*, Cistercian Publications, Kalamazoo, Michigan, 1981, Vol. 2, p. 142.

CHAPTER 6

Travellers and wanderers

The fourth century was a period of great social change, and the life of Egypt was affected by it as most other areas in the Roman empire were. Already in the large numbers who travelled up or down the Nile to Pachomius we find people of different origins, speaking different dialects and different languages. As must have happened in the Roman army with men of different races each group was accommodated separately at Tabennisi, and each was given instruction in their own language. The Greek influence was already strong in Egypt, dating from the founding of the Greek colony in Alexandria by Alexander the Great. It was this growing influence which led to the decline in the original Coptic genius for simple and humble living, largely illiterate, to a Greek passion for speculative theology. The Greek idea that union with God was primarily intellectual led to a very different emphasis in the monastic life, away from simple praxis to the heady delights of scholarship.

Theological controversies raged; particularly disruptive in Egypt was the rise of what was later known as the Arian heresy. The Council of Nicaea in 325 was supposed to have settled the matter of theological orthodoxy, but controversy continued. Arius was a priest in Alexandria, by some accounts a Libyan by birth. Athanasius, the champion of orthodoxy, came from the Greek Alexandrian community, and was appointed bishop of Alexandria shortly after the council of Nicaea. Immediately he came into conflict with the Arian party, who had powerful friends in Rome. He was deposed and exiled to Trier, on the River Moselle, at that time the administrative centre from which Gaul, Britain and Spain were ruled, and the favourite residence of the

Emperor Constantine the Great. It was described by the Roman poet Ausonius as "Rome beyond the Alps", so that Athanasius was not banished to a wilderness. While there he made a number of missionary journeys. After a year he returned to Alexandria but was forced to flee again in 339, when he travelled to Rome, bringing with him two Egyptian monks, who caused a stir in Roman Christian society. Athanasius' role as a champion of orthodoxy led to further periods of exile; in 356 he escaped to Upper Egypt, finding shelter in the numerous monasteries there. Athanasius had always been a zealous promoter of monasticism, and had known Pachomius and Antony, whose life he wrote in about 357, and which had a great influence on the spread of monasticism. Orthodoxy finally triumphed at the Council of Constantinople in 381.

Athanasius' 'Life of Antony' was of course propaganda, and had great influence, and he probably promoted the monastic life in his frequent travels in Gaul and Italy. We have a glimpse of his influence in the 'Confessions' of Augustine[1] which tells us of a visit in 386, at a time when Augustine was struggling with his vocation, of Pontitianus, a friend who held high office in the emperor's court. He discovered that Augustine had beside him a copy of the letters of the Apostle Paul, and told him about Antony and the monks of Egypt. He also gave an account of an afternoon at Trier, when the emperor was taken up with the Circensian games and he and three others in the emperor's service went for a walk in gardens near the city walls. He paired off with one of them and the other two found a little house containing a small group of ascetics. There they came across a copy of the Life of Antony. As one of them began to read it, he turned to his friend and said, "'What are we looking for in what we are doing? What is our motive in being in the public service? Do we have any higher hope at court than to be friends of the emperor? And at that level, is not everything uncertain and full of dangers? And how many other hazards must we meet on the way to this dangerous position? And how long will it be before we get there? But if I should choose to be a friend of God, I can become one straight away.' And as he spoke, troubled with the pain of the new life coming to birth in him, he turned his eyes back to the book." And both men decided to remain there with the ascetics.

Despite the impact of the 'Life of Antony' in educated circles it was not the whole story. The monastic movement has a momentum of its own, and although history shows us certain recognisable figures, the countless unknown and shadowy ones are the silent ones who went on faithfully living the life in one form or another without the spotlight falling upon them. But the organisers and the innovators are those who have left traces behind them. The first record we have of the solitary life in Roman Gaul is that of Martin. After some years as a soldier in the Roman army he became a hermit, living on an island in the Mediterranean. In 360, fourteen years after the death of Antony, he established a semi-eremitical monastery at Ligugé, near Poitiers, whose bishop Hilary was his friend. In 371 he was chosen bishop by popular acclaim of the people of Tours. Despite his labours as a bishop he remained fundamentally a monk, and established a monastery at Marmoutier, about two miles from Tours, where he led the eremitical life. His cell was a wooden hut; he had some eighty disciples, most of whom lived in caves hollowed out of rocks in the cliff. The life led resembled that of the Egyptian desert. Other solitaries in France, whose lives and traditions were recorded by Gregory of Tours some two hundred years later, lived in the same desert style.

On the French Mediterranean coast, opposite Cannes, lies the island of Lérins, where in 410 a monk called Honoratus arrived with a companion. The island was infested, as usual, with snakes and scorpions which of course promptly left. In his youth Honoratus had travelled in Greece and other parts of the East, studying the monastic life. Other solitaries joined them; the life was semi-eremitical, with monks meeting together in church for a common office. As was usual in the eremitical tradition there was no written rule; the teaching was oral. Some distance from the monastery, possibly on an adjacent island, were other cells where lived others who chose greater solitude. Lérins became a place of training and many of the hermits of Lérins became bishops. Even England was influenced by it in the person of Benedict Biscop (c. 628-690), the founder of the monastery of St Peter at Wearmouth and of St Paul at Jarrow, where Bede wrote his History of the English Church and People. Benedict Biscop lived as a monk at Lérins for two years, 665-667.

Of these early pioneers of the monastic life outside Egypt none was more influential than John Cassian (c. 360-c. 435), probably a native of Gaul who spent the early part of his life in a monastery in Bethlehem. With his friend Germanus he visited Egypt and spent some years amongst the ascetics of the desert. In about 415 he returned to Gaul and founded two monasteries, one for women and one for men, both coenobitic, at Marseilles. Cassian was the first systematiser of the monastic life; at the request of a neighbouring bishop who wished to introduce the monastic life into his area, he wrote his 'Institutes', a description of the dress, food, and disciplines of monastic life in the East. His aim was to adapt this life to the West.

A little later he wrote his 'Conferences', accounts of the teachings of the great spiritual masters of Egypt. The second book of the 'Conferences' was dedicated to Honoratus of Lérins, who afterwards became bishop of Arles. Both the Institutes and the Conferences have been a great influence on the formation of monastic life in the West; large portions of the Rule of St Benedict were based on Cassian's writings. Benedict's famous category of three sorts of monks, coenobites, anchorites and Sarabaites[2] comes straight from Conference XVII of Cassian. Although his chief interest in his travels through the Egyptian desert was in the solitary life, Cassian came to believe that no-one could undertake this life without a preliminary training, which was what the coenobium was intended to provide. Benedict himself speaks of the coenobium as "a school of the Lord's service";[3] later ages were to take the school days as the norm, rather than something to be grown out of. The solitary life which Benedict presents as the crown of the monastic life was forgotten.

Since all these developments in Gaul were in areas which had been colonised by the Romans for several hundred years, communications were easy. Ideas became part of the intellectual climate of the time and spread rapidly. Books were copied and distributed, every monastery would have had a scriptorium for the copying of the Bible and other books. In Gaul Christianity was typically centred in the towns which were Roman settlements; the Celtic people of Gaul did not live in towns but in scattered groups, following their traditional way of life. It is not surprising then that Christianity was seen as emanating from Rome and taking a definitive Roman shape. Bishops, with their seats in major towns, became authoritative figures in Roman society, administering their districts as Roman governors would do. In the figure of Martin we still have traces of an older charismatic authority from the desert; it is significant that his biographer Sulpicius Severus who from his name clearly identifies himself with Rome, depicts Martin as a thaumaturge and wonder-worker. Martin's authority does not derive from Roman power-structures but from some other power.

In 314 the Emperor Constantine summoned the first general council of his western half of the empire to meet at Arles. Some thirty-three bishops attended, among them three from Britain, the bishops of York, London and probably Lincoln. This shows that the Roman system of town bishops was already in place in Britain. Significantly they are all three from the eastern and more Romanised part of Britain, but Christianity must have already been well-established there for bishops to have appeared only a year or so after Constantine's official edict of toleration in 313. It was only some ten years since the emperor Diocletian had ordered all Christians to be savagely persecuted; the names of Alban and the hermits Julius and Aaron of

Caerleon have been remembered as martyrs of Britain from this time, according to Bede,[4] although modern scholars have suggested that the story of Alban comes from an earlier wave of persecution in 209. There are references to a Christian presence in Britain in the writings of Tertullian and Origen in the early part of the third century.

But Christianity did not come to Britain with the Romans, who were mainly pagans although there may have been a few believers in their ranks. This is something that the earlier generation of historians, with their reverence for the classical world and all things Roman found hard to believe. The poverty of the British bishops was remarked upon at Arles; Christianity in Britain was not the faith of the ruling classes but of ordinary people. It is very probable that it arrived in the Romanised areas from Gaul, brought by Christian missionaries.

But Christianity as it appeared in the western, unromanised part of the British Isles was very different. It was monastic in form, like the Christianity of the eastern Mediterranean. The Glastonbury legends may point to the probability that it arrived in Britain by sea by means of trade routes. We know that traders from the Mediterranean came to Britain in search of tin, iron, lead, copper, silver and gold, and of such things as hides and slaves, and hunting dogs. Since Celtic Britain did not have a money economy, although some rulers did issue coins, they would be bartered for fine pottery, textiles, wine and oil. These trade routes were established in prehistoric times, and have been traced by modern archaeologists who have studied the remains of Mediterranean artefacts, discovered round the western coasts of Britain, which have even included glass from Egypt.[5] Most of these trade routes were to the west of Britain, which was where the mineral deposits were. In these places, the Celtic tribal areas still largely untouched by the Roman military superstructure which governed by means of pacts with tribal rulers, first appeared other Christian missionaries. These men were monks who led a semi-eremitical life.

The Celts were great seafarers, and there was frequent coming and going across the Celtic sea between Wales, Ireland and Strathclyde, as well as other Celtic regions such as Cornwall and Brittany. The early missionaries, the *peregrini* or wanderers, either alone or in a small group would travel until they found a suitable place for settlement. Some even went as far as the Faroes and Iceland. *Xeniteia*, the wandering of one who was a stranger and pilgrim on earth, was a lifestyle already known in Egypt; Cassian's early life was that of a wanderer as he journeyed from monastery to monastery in Egypt and in other places in his subsequent career before he finally came to a settled Roman way of life in Marseilles. Between the fourth and sixth centuries wandering Irish monks, the *peregrini* who evangelised Europe, continued a tradition which first came from the eastern Mediterranean. To leave home, as they did, for the love of God was the equivalent of going into the desert, separating themselves from their family and their native land. It could be that the fourth class of monks so condemned by Benedict, the *girovagi*, ever roaming with no stability, might have been Irish monks who made settlements at Bobbio and other places in Italy. This wandering lifestyle is of course quite normal in Hindu monasticism, with the figure of the sannyasi, and it surfaced in another form in the later Mendicant orders of friars. Such a lifestyle has ample apostolic precedent in the scriptures, but something so unregulated was bound to offend Roman sensibilities.

Celtic monasticism retained the primitive way of life of the early hermits of the desert. As monasteries grew in size individuals or small groups would move into seclusion, very often on islands in lakes or rivers, or off the coast. Nearly every island round the coasts of the British Isles had at one time a hermit living on it. This eremitical pattern was very different from the way later monasticism developed in the West. This received its characteristic form from the 'Western Patriarch', Benedict of Nursia (c. 480-c. 550). Benedict was educated in Rome where, it is said, the licentiousness of Roman society led him at about the age of twenty to withdraw into the life of a hermit in a cave at Subiaco. Here he spent some years until, like Antony, he acquired followers. Unlike Antony however he founded monasteries, eventually in about 525 moving to Monte Cassino, where he remained until his death. His Rule is notable for its breadth and toleration, as he described it, "a little rule for beginners".[6] As we have seen, a rule to be obeyed by all is the means by which the coenobium, or community, is governed. In the Rule of St Benedict authority is vested in the abbot, who is no longer the charismatic figure of the desert abba but one invested with the divine authority of the Byzantine *pantocrator*. Obedience is the main virtue of the coenobitic monk, since all authority comes from above, whence grace trickles down to the lower levels.

By assimilating monks to the Roman system of authority Benedict effectually suppressed the free-range nature of the monk as wanderer and prophet with the emphasis of the Benedictine vows of stability, obedience and conversion of life. Separateness was now that of the separate community, withdrawn from the world, a way of life which ran parallel to the world but not involved in it. The uncertainties of the solitary life, the responsibility for one's own salvation, were effectively removed by the vow of obedience, which was the final resource in all doubtful areas.[7] It was something which met the needs of the time. Rome had been sacked by the Vandals, barbarian tribes from the northeast, in 455, only some twenty-five years before Benedict was born, and the old Roman certainties had crumbled. The whole Roman empire was under threat from these new peoples. The last Roman emperor abdicated in 475.

Britain too was affected by the withdrawal of Roman troops to defend the seat of empire. Pagan Saxon tribes invaded the south-east; by the end of the fifth century they controlled all eastern Britain as far as the Humber, and a hundred years later the West Saxons pushed into Wiltshire and the upper part of the Thames Valley, together with the country beyond as far as the Severn, and gradually extended their conquests. Only Wales, Cornwall and

Scotland, the ancient Celtic areas, were unaffected. In 596 Pope Gregory the Great, an ardent promoter of Benedictine monasticism and himself a monk, dispatched Augustine, prior of his own monastery of St Andrew in Rome, on a mission to the pagan Saxons of Kent. He was received favourably by Ethelbert, king of Kent, whose wife Bertha was a Christian. Within a few months Ethelbert formally adopted Christianity, and Augustine went to Arles to be consecrated as Archbishop of Canterbury. In 598 Augustine established a monastery at Canterbury, dedicated to St Peter and St Paul.

Augustine seems to have been a man of somewhat limited intelligence and spiritual capacity. He wrote to Gregory for direction on the smallest points. Gregory had loftily given him jurisdiction (that great Roman power) over the whole of Britain, though his specific mission was to the pagan Saxons. He became aware that outside the Saxon areas there were other Christians, and in about 603 with the assistance of Ethelbert he attempted to reach agreement with them. Bede gives us an account of what happened at the arranged meeting place, probably at Aust on the south bank of the river Severn, where the Severn bridge now starts for Wales. Until the bridge was built there had been a ferry at this place for several thousand years.

The British bishops crossed the river in their coracles to meet Augustine. Like him, they were monks, but from a very different tradition. Bede tells us that there were seven bishops, not territorial bishops after the Roman model, but monastics, and many learned men, who came mainly from the monastery at Bangor in north Wales. This monastery, Bede informs us, was a vast place, divided into seven sections, each under its own abbot, with three hundred monks apiece, all of whom supported themselves by manual work. Before the meeting they had consulted a wise and prudent hermit about what they should do. He told them that if Augustine rose to greet them when they met he was a servant of Christ and they should come to an agreement with him. But Augustine remained seated, and they correctly perceived that he wished to rule them and departed without reaching agreement.[8]

This story shows the confrontation of two monastic traditions. For Bede of course, the great Romaniser, the British church was holy but wrong, wearing the wrong sort of tonsure (the British monks shaved the front part of their heads, as the Druid priests had before them) and wholly misguided as to the correct date for Easter. It was inevitable that the Romanisers eventually won this argument at the Synod of Whitby in 664. Colman, the Bishop of Lindisfarne, the great Celtic monastic centre, returned sadly to his native Ireland (he had originally been a monk of Iona and at the Synod had appealed to the authority of St Columba). But it would be several hundred years before the Celtic Church was finally defeated, and the faith of the old Celtic areas still has a very different style from that of the areas colonized by the Romans.

The Saxons, once converted, became enthusiastic promoters of Benedictine monasticism, and built great abbeys at places like Shaftesbury and Malmesbury, which had been a monastery founded by the Irish hermit Maeldubh. Aldhelm, his pupil, became Bishop of Sherborne in 705, and an advocate of the new style of church government. But as we shall see, the solitary way of life was not so easily suppressed.

NOTES

1. Augustine, *Confessions*, Book 8, 14-15.
2. *Rule of St Benedict*, 1.
3. *Ibid.*, Prologue.
4. Bede, *Eccl. Hist.*, I. 7.
5. See E.R. Bowen, *Saints, Seaways and Settlements*, University of Wales Press, 1969.
6. *Rule of St Benedict*, 73.
7. *Ibid.*, 58.
8. Bede, *Eccl. Hist.*, II. 2. History might have been very different had Augustine possessed the diplomatic skills and biblical awareness of Pope John XXIII who, some fourteen centuries later, was to embrace the representatives of other Churches with the words, "Behold Joseph your brother".

CHAPTER 7

Institutions and hermits

As the Saxons found, and as the Normans were to follow, Benedictine monasticism provided the perfect religious buttress for a developing and prosperous society. Church and State went hand in hand as they were to continue to do until a thousand years later the Reformation was to redistribute the power ratio. From a demographic standpoint the monastic life was an instrument of social control, keeping down the growth of population, providing a way of life for many who would not otherwise be provided for, and a window of opportunity for those of ability and scholarly tastes to make their mark. For surplus royal ladies it provided in the role of abbess a position befitting their rank and an opportunity to exercise power. For them and for other women it provided an alternative to the only role that the society of the time offered; that of wife and mother. For many women it offered the possibility of an educated and cultured life not otherwise attainable. The monasteries also had an important role in caring for the poor of society.

Monasticism as an alternative society became established within the feudal system with its elaborate networks of interdependent obligations. Both abbots and bishops were feudal lords and were drawn from the ruling classes; as feudal lords they were expected to provide fighting men in times of war, and often bishops were expected to lead their troops into battle. The monks were the praying part of society, a service that they rendered on behalf of others. The Benedictine *opus Dei*, the ceaseless round of the Office continued night and day, while other people were occupied with mundane affairs. The Benedictine emphasis was upon the life of the family living in peace and harmony rather than upon individual striving; bodily austerity and the eremitical life were in effect discarded.

Nevertheless there were some Benedictine solitaries, those who in Benedict's words "not in the first fervour of religious life, but after long probation in the monastery, have learned by the help and experience of many to fight against the devil; and going forth well armed from the ranks of their brethren to the single-handed combat of the desert, are able, without the support of others, to fight by the strength of their own arm, God helping them, against the vices of the flesh and their evil thoughts."[1] Many Benedictine monasteries in various parts of Europe had groups of solitaries attached to them, Montserrat in Spain and many others. Even Iona, since 1203 under Benedictine rule, continued the eremitical tradition first brought there by Columba in 563. These solitaries said the Office, in solidarity with their brethren, at the ringing of a bell, alone in their cells. Various small congregations of hermits, such as that of Fonte Avellana under Peter Damian (1007-1072), whose rule attempted to restore the austerity of the Egyptian desert, finally reverted to being purely coenobitical. The Italian Benedictine congregations of Olivetans and Silvestrines, founded in the thirteenth century, re-emphasised the solitary nature of a monk's life. This vocation to solitude survived within the coenobitic way of life, receiving emphasis from time to time in the use of the cowl, or in the total silence of the Trappists, now no longer observed. But the Benedictine rule is designed for coenobites, not for solitaries, whose traditions are different.

The Cistercians, who began as a community of hermits following the Benedictine Rule in the forest of Molesmes in the late eleventh century, chose solitude by removing themselves to uninhabited places, away from towns, where they restored Benedict's primitive emphasis on manual labour and simplicity of life. The Order had particular success in Wales, where it appealed more to the Celtic love of nature and wild places than Benedictinism which, with its urban emphasis, was entirely English and associated with the hated foreign invaders.[2] The life was coenobitic, and solitude having been built in to their way of life, individual hermits have been discouraged, a tradition that Thomas Merton struggled against.

St Romuald (d. 1027), founder of the Camaldolese order, spent most of his life as a wandering hermit. He started as a Benedictine but after three years left to place himself under the direction of a hermit, where three others joined them. After some years of wandering he was offered some land in Tuscany, where he was joined by five others. The life established there was semi-eremitic, the monks living in separate cells and meeting in church for the Divine Office. After two years St Romuald set off once more on his travels, pausing to establish another austere monastic settlement at Sitria, near Sassoferrato, before moving on. But by the end of the fifteenth century all but one of the monasteries of the Camaldolese order had abandoned the solitary life, when the reforms of Paolo Giustiniani gave it a new congregation of hermits which he called The Company of St Romuald.

The most lasting experiment in the institutional solitary life has been that of the Carthusians, founded by St Bruno (c. 1030-1101). His original foundation, that of La Grande Chartreuse, nowadays a stop on the tourist trail, was in those days inaccessible and remote, and far from the influence of town life. This lonely and silent place, where snow lay for some six months of the year was where Bruno and his small band of solitaries built their wooden huts, one hut for two men, and their tiny chapel. Here they lived the life of the Egyptian desert, in silence, reading, prayer and manual labour. St Bruno, in true eremitical tradition, never drew up a written Rule or had any intention of founding an Order, in terms of canon law; some years after his death his followers described themselves in the heading of a letter addressed to the monks of Cluny, as "Christ's poor men who dwell in the desert of the Chartreuse for love of the Name of Jesus".

The later way of life of the Carthusians still retained this spirit. The cell of the modern Carthusian is a small self-contained cottage where all activities are carried out, and meals are eaten. Only on Sundays and on great festivals do the community eat together in the refectory. At the appointed hours, at the sound of a bell, the Divine Office is recited by each monk in his cell. The Night Office is sung in church, as is Mass the following morning. Once a week the whole community take a walk together outside the enclosure of the monastery.

The first foundation of Carthusians in England was made at Witham in the Mendips in 1175-6 by Henry II, who appointed Hugh, later bishop of Lincoln, as its prior. In medieval times nine Charterhouses were founded in England. In the fifteenth century the highest number of Charterhouses in Europe reached one hundred and ninety. There were also Carthusian nuns, who became quite numerous in the Middle Ages.

As early as the third century, so tradition says, there were Christian hermits on Mount Carmel, a chain of mountains running from north-west to south-east in northern Palestine. Here the prophet Elijah's cave is still venerated; there is a long tradition of hermits going back some nine hundred years before the Christian era, living in the many caves in the mountains. Late in the twelfth century the Christian hermits were, in the medieval manner, organised and given a rule. After the fall of Jerusalem in 1187 the number of solitaries greatly increased but the country had become more and more dangerous for Christians to live in. Some hermits left the mountain and settled in France, and some came soon afterwards to England, where they settled near Cambridge. Soon the primitive eremitical life was abandoned for a coenobitic one. Early in the fifteenth century the first convents of Carmelite nuns were founded and within a hundred years the Order had spread all over Europe, becoming particularly rooted in Spain. The Primitive Rule had largely been abandoned when St Teresa and St John of the Cross started their reforms. Their first house was opened in 1568, and the constitutions, drawn up by St

Teresa herself in virtue of a brief granted her by Pope Pius IV in 1565, were finally approved in 1581.

In these constitutions special emphasis was laid upon the contemplative character of the Order, making provision for the building of hermitages to which the brethren can retire "according to the custom of our holy fathers". But there arose a certain division in the Order since the Carmelite vocation had been that of missionary work since arriving in Europe. St Thérèse of Lisieux, a later Carmelite saint, is seen as the patron of missions. Those in hermitages abandoned missionary work for a life of contemplation. The division was resolved by the establishment of 'desert' convents, where any members of the Order could retire from time to time to live the solitary life. The normal period of residence was to be a year; many friars after four or five years of active mission work would return to the desert. The typical desert community was of around twenty members, governed by a prior capable of giving spiritual direction and help to the members. The hermits lived in separate cells, in poverty and simplicity, eating together and meeting in church for the usual office. In addition to the main building, there were a number of separate hermitages in the woods, as laid down by St Teresa's reform, consisting of two or three rooms and a chapel, and surrounded by a wall. Now and again the occupants of the main building would retire to one of these hermitages for a given period, each friar taking with him enough food to last for a week. He had to follow the same rule of life as in the main convent, having to ring his bell in response to the main bell, and recite the Office at the same time. From time to time the prior would visit the solitaries in their cells.

The Carmelites are termed friars, or Mendicants, which term is also applied to the Franciscans and Dominicans. Unlike monks, their allegiance is to their Order rather than to a particular place, which means that they can travel around as their work calls them. The wandering life, as we have seen, was adopted very early by certain groups seeking to separate themselves from their families and native place. St Francis of Assisi's embracing of poverty was an expression of separation from possessions and ties of all sorts. The early followers of Francis had no settled abode; they wandered about preaching and passed the night in haylofts or church porches, following the one who had nowhere to lay his head (Mt 8:20). Here and there they established small hermitages, or little solitudes, where they might withdraw for rest and prayer. St Francis himself had been divided between the life of a hermit and that of a wandering preacher. Alas, after Francis' death the Order, as it had become, split into two, divided between those who wished to maintain the primitive discipline and those who wished to hold property, building large monasteries in towns and magnificent churches such as the Basilica of San Francesco at Assisi. Some three hundred years later the Capuchin reform attempted to restore the eremitical life. The first hermits lived in strict poverty in wattle huts, sleeping upon the ground, wearing habits of the coarsest material and going barefoot even in winter. But before very long the solitude was abandoned and the friars settled in or near large towns where alms were more readily obtainable, and while still retaining much of their primitive austerity, took up an active life of mission work and preaching. There were in addition many members of the Third Order of St Francis who adopted a life of solitude, the best known of them perhaps being Ramon Lull (1232-1315), poet, philosopher and apostle to the Muslims.

The Dominicans were another preaching order with a contemplative basis. St Dominic himself, a contemporary of St Francis, spent long periods alone in prayer. There have been Dominican solitaries, particularly among the tertiaries, among them St Catherine of Siena who spent three years in solitude and silence before beginning an active apostolate, and St Rose of Lima.

There were many other congregations of hermits, living a semi-eremitical life, defined by the provisions of canon law and governed by an approved Rule. The hermit way of life has always been seen by the institutional Church as a threat to good order and the legitimate possession of property. Such an unaccountable way of life must be strictly regulated and brought under central control. But for nearly two thousand years there have been those Christians called to a solitary life who have lived in a way not subject to official regulation, living individual lives of devotion and holiness, hidden and unknown. These may be called the invisible ones, whose existence has been recognised by ordinary people but often not by the official channels of the Church. These people have felt called to live in solitude, not primarily to join any form of officially recognised religious life. This call to solitude may be termed the original monastic vocation, before it acquired the trappings of the medieval idea of 'states of life'.

Before the Reformation such a way of life was widespread. In England alone there is evidence of at least 1000 known cells, and the actual names of over 650 anchorites and hermits have been discovered.[3] This was really a survival of the ancient Celtic eremitical way of life before living in towns had been adopted, as described by Giraldus Cambrensis: "They do not live in towns, villages or castles, but lead a solitary existence, deep in the woods".[4] Such hermits and anchorites were ordinary laypeople, both men and women, and they were fully accepted as a part of medieval society without being in any way regarded as odd. As laypeople they were not regulated by canon law, and earned their living by keeping roads and bridges in repair, or by maintaining lighthouses, clearing waste places and various public works, or preaching and teaching and taking charge of chapels. Even in the cities there were hermits; in London there was a famous hermit in the Tower of London, and another who lived in London Wall.

There was a great upsurge in the eremitical life in the twelfth century, probably as a reaction to the increased formalisation and regulation of the monastic life. Many hermits went to live in the forests which in those days still covered most of the land. In Russia such a way of life has continued up until modern times in the *taiga* or primal forest. Such hermits were held in great honour; in the *Liber Vitae* of Durham Cathedral, 'ancres' were ranked above abbots and other ecclesiastical dignitaries. We know the names of some of the most famous ones: Godric of Finchale, once a sea-rover, Christina of Markyate, Wulfric of Haselbury, and many others. Richard Rolle, the hermit of Hampole, who ran away from home to be a hermit as others might run away to sea, begged two of his sister's dresses to make himself a hermit's habit.[5] Adopting such a habit was a sufficient sign without having to go through any particular channels of authorisation. No doubt a few rogues and vagabonds adopted it too, as a way of receiving alms to support themselves.

The anchorites, whose name derives from the Greek word *anachoretes*, meaning one who goes apart, were an authorised category. Both men and women were anchorites, and in the Middle Ages having an 'anker' living in your church was a status symbol, rather like having a BMW in the garage today. Many churches still bear traces of such occupation, sometimes only in the form of a squint in the outside wall, although subsequent rebuilding has removed many clues. The anchorhouse was usually built in the churchyard against the wall of the church, sometimes in stone, in which case they may have survived, although others may have been less permanent constructions of timber and plaster. A small courtyard or enclosed garden may have been added.

"Recluses dwell under the eaves of the church", says the Ancrene Wisse, an early thirteenth century treatise, "because they understand that they should be of so holy a life that the whole of Holy Church, that is, Christian people, can lean upon them and trust them, while they hold her up with their holiness of life and blessed prayers. This is why an anchoress is called an anchoress, and is anchored under a church like an anchor under the side of a ship, to hold that ship so that waves and storms do not overturn it."[6]

The life of the anchorite, or recluse, was the most demanding of all, a voluntary imprisonment or living death.

With the experiences of middle eastern hostages still fresh in our minds we are most likely to see enclosure in negative terms, but with the emphasis which arose in the twelfth century upon the human nature of Christ such a way of life was seen as a sharing of the sufferings of Christ upon the cross. "All you ever endure is penance," says the Ancrene Wisse, "and hard penance my dear sisters; all the good you ever do, all you suffer, is martyrdom for you in the most severe of orders, for night and day you are up on God's cross".[7]

It was a life as heroic as that of the early ascetics of the desert. Some who chose this way of life were professed religious, seeking deeper seclusion, but most were ordinary laypeople. It was not something that could be borne by the merely eccentric or immature, since one could spend forty years or more in such seclusion, as did Julian of Norwich, perhaps the most widely known medieval recluse today. Unlike hermits, who might or might not have official approval of their life, the anchorite was officially enclosed with a special rite by the local bishop. A woman living alone without the protection of a man had to receive official status and the protection of the church, after careful investigation of her character and of the provision made for her support, sometimes from her own resources but often by a local landowner who acquired merit thereby. A religious would have the support of his or her own community.

The earliest complete instruction on the anchoretic way of life was that written by Aelred of Rievaulx (1109-1167) for his sister, who had already been an ancre for some years. It is of particular interest for being based in scholarly fashion upon the writings of the Fathers, and upon traditions of monastic solitude different from that of the Benedictine rule which Aelred himself must have followed. "De Institutione Inclusarum" was written in Latin, and we do not know if his sister could read it herself, since in those days most women were "illiterate", which meant that they knew no Latin, though they might be able to read and write in their own tongue. Ancrene Wisse (broadly translated as

"How to be an Ancre"), which followed some fifty years or so later, draws upon Aelred, but it is written in the vernacular specifically for women, three sisters, it is believed, who lived together in Herefordshire. It is a brilliant work of spiritual and practical guidance, and gives a remarkably clear picture of the life of a recluse in the thirteenth century.

The dwelling consisted of three rooms, mainly the cell, containing an altar covered with a white linen cloth and carrying a crucifix, together with a bed and other furniture. There were three windows, which were the recluse's only contact with the world outside, one looking into the church, one into the house and one into the parlour. The parlour window was normally closed by a shutter and a curtain of black cloth with a white cross upon it. From behind this curtain she could converse with anyone who came to seek her counsel, and with her confessor and spiritual guide. Through the third window she could converse with her servants. She was to have two maids, one of whom was to remain in the house at all times while the other could go out when necessary. The anchoress was to keep no cattle or other animals to draw her heart outwards, except for a cat, in those days a necessity for keeping down the rats and mice but no doubt also a welcome companion.

The Ancrene Wisse contains many warnings against "peeping anchoresses", those who love their windows too much and turn their attention to external things rather than the interior life of prayer to which they are committed. Such a life may seem to be an imprisonment, with its sensory deprivation and its lack of exercise and fresh air. But it was a life freely chosen; a cell is only a prison under necessity. Lest it be thought that such a life is a peculiarity of the medieval past it may come as a surprise to learn that there are those today who live a completely reclusive life, although not in the church building but usually in the context of a religious community, who can supply the necessities of life. It is of course a life of complete dependence upon others, and many modern solitaries feel that this dependence reflects the structures of medieval society rather than that of today. Those who follow a solitary vocation today are more likely to follow the ancient monastic precedent of working for a living, like the monks of the desert who wove mats and baskets and sold them in the market place.

With the religious upheavals of the sixteenth century the monastic life of England came to an end, taking with it the recognised eremitical life. But there were still solitaries although they no longer had a visible presence in society. The tradition of the solitary life was still remembered however; Dr Johnson said "I never read of a hermit but in imagination I kiss his feet."

NOTES

1. *Rule of St Benedict*, 1.
2. See David H. Williams, *The Welsh Cistercians*, 2 vols., Caldey Island 1984.
3. See: R.M. Clay, *Hermits and Anchorites of England*, London 1912.
4. Giraldus Cambrensis, *Descriptio Kambriae*, 1, 17.
5. Richard Rolle of Hampole, *Legenda* compiled by the nuns of Hampole, quoted by Clifton Wolters in the Introduction to his translation of 'The Fire of Love', Penguin Books.
6. *Ancrene Wisse*, iii.
7. *Ibid.*, iv.

PART 3
THE CHRISTIAN SOLITARY

CHAPTER 8

The Christian solitary: a new vocation?

In the preceding two or three chapters we have had a brief look at the foundations of two thousand years of Christian monastic history. Monastic movements rise and decline but the patterns of life remain remarkably constant, the tension between solitude and the need to pass on the manner of life which has been found fruitful by those following a particular path. Always there are the charisms of those who are called to reform and renew existing patterns. These are people possessed not so much by a desire or talent for reorganisation, though they may have had this talent, as by a fresh vision of what monasticism is all about.

Monasticism has taken on many forms, and has been combined with many other activities, such as philosophy, scholarship, scientific research, poetry, painting and other things for which the life has been a setting rather than a stimulus. It provided a stable basis for those who chose these pursuits. But in our days monasticism, like many other institutions of society, is in apparent decline. Anyone with any knowledge of the history of monasticism will not therefore write it off, as something belonging to the medieval past, but know that a sudden reversal of its fortunes may happen at any time. As a witness to another way of life from that commonly accepted in our present era it must have a future. It still maintains its witness to separation from the values of society, quietly pursuing its own tradition.

What is being shed are the accidental accretions acquired by monasticism throughout history and particularly in the recent past. The vast buildings, the wealth, the security from all possibilities of poverty and homelessness which insulated the religious orders from the life of the poor who cast themselves daily upon God's providence and with whom the early monks identified themselves, have been brought into question by economic pressures as much as anything else. Also questioned has been the élitism of those accorded a privileged place within the Church. Monasticism, in order to speak with its original prophetic voice, has to detach itself from its accommodations with a society which is founded upon power, privilege and the consumption of the world's resources. It has to rediscover the insecurity which is the lot of ordinary working people today.

Such a renewal will come from below, not from a process of cutting one's losses, moving to smaller buildings and moving out into 'the world'. The monastic witness is one of a dependence upon God alone, not one of living like anyone else with a few prayers added. Without this radical and total dependence upon God true monastic life is not possible. This dependence is what marks the separation of the monk within society, not the wearing of a habit or living in a special place.

What marks off the monk from other groups seeking a dedicated lifestyle is that the aim of the monk is not the formation of 'community', in the way that others currently perceive their objective. Living by rule is a means, not an end. Living with others is for the monk an ascetic tool in the journey towards God alone, a means by which attachment to one's own will and desires can be perceived and overcome.

What has been happening in recent years, as institutional monasticism has been declining, is a remarkable resurgence of the call to solitude. Within the monasteries there has been provision made for St Benedict's "second class of monks; those who not in the first fervour of religious life... [go] forth well-armed from the ranks of their brethren to the single-handed combat of the desert...",[1] in the form of a moving out of some men and women into hermitages of various sorts. But this call to solitude has also been occurring amongst ordinary people living ordinary lives, often with no connections with the monastic tradition. Often such people are puzzled by this strange impulse to seek solitude, not only to be alone but to be separated in some way from the aims and values of society which become tasteless and meaningless. As we have seen, this call is nothing new; it has been experienced in many times and in many places. But it would seem that today this call is being felt more and more strongly by many people.

The idea of 'vocation' has until now been identified with a call to be something specific, such as a nun or a priest. The word 'vocation' is just a Latinism for the English word 'call'; as commonly used it assumes that somewhere out there, there is a special niche prepared into which we can enter, providing that we fulfil the necessary criteria. Such a view springs from the concept of the Church as institution, into which people are fitted, and which like the facades of medieval cathedrals present a prepared face to the world.

The Churches of the Reformation abandoned the idea of vocation being selective, replacing it with the idea that all Christian people had one vocation by virtue of their baptism. This is an idea which the old monks would not have disagreed with, seeing their call as being to the fullness of baptismal life, not to a special place in society. So the monasteries were closed, their inhabitants dispersed, and their poor dependants abandoned to private charity, a process which is not unfamiliar today, and rigorism became the province of the Puritan faction.

But the call which so many ordinary people feel today seems to point them beyond the role of being a church worker or helper to something more demanding for which the institutional Church has nothing to offer, it seems, apart from a provision in Roman Catholic canon law[2] for laypeople to live according to rule, and which involves celibacy. For such a call to come to someone living an ordinary life with clear obligations to other people which cannot be abandoned can be puzzling. Something is being asked, by a voice which is insistent and demanding, but just what this is does not appear clearly.

This is of course the pattern which appears in the Bible; Moses was just minding his father-in-law's sheep in the usual way on the slopes of Mount Horeb when he saw a bush blazing with fire (Ex 3:1-6). When he went to find out why he heard his name called. His response, "Here I am", his yes, led him into further and further demands being made upon him. So it is with the prophets; a demand is made to which they respond. They are not given a special place in society but a task to fulfil, a task which will unfold gradually.

God's call can come to anyone, at any time, and in any circumstances. It is not easy to understand this call and how it is worked out in one's life. Sometimes one can only stand, like Moses on Mount Pisgah, and look back at the miles of desert one has crossed. It does not come gift-wrapped, with a label attached, but in fragments, more like a jigsaw puzzle, to be painfully pieced together, and gradually asking more and more of us. It may be quite late in one's life-journey before one recognises it for what it is. Before this point it may be felt merely as an emptiness, an absence.

The call to solitude is the primary monastic vocation, without the historically conditioned accompaniments. It may come as an enormous relief to discover that this call which puts one's life in some way out of joint, which draws one to the fringes of the desert where unknown vastnesses stretch ahead, is something which many people in the past have experienced and which many people experience today. The call is by name, it is personal and individual and not just a matter of finding a slot to fit into. The response to the call is also personal and individual; our personality, needs and background will shape our path. It is rather like falling in love; entering a relationship which gives meaning to our life. Who knows where it will lead?

In the Middle Ages it was a social commonplace that

people could experience this interior call and withdraw themselves from society for a life of prayer. They were not regarded as particularly odd but as those who could intercede for the sins of others. They lived humbly, supporting themselves with work, with probably the occasional food being offered them by those who asked for their counsel and prayers. What function does the solitary fulfil in society today?

The solitary is first of all a useless person. This in itself is remarkable in a society where everyone is rated by their occupation or activity. The call of the solitary is not to be anything, to have any sort of public persona or mask. It is rather to be totally available to God, to live a hidden life of solitude. It is a call to share in the profound solitude of God, in the depths of the mystery of God's being. The world refuses this solitude, the God who is wholly other from the world's concerns, the one who calls us beyond those concerns into the divine mystery. Even the incarnation is an inconceivable mystery, according to the seventh century theologian Maximus the Confessor: "By taking flesh God makes himself understood only by appearing still more incomprehensible. He remains hidden... even in this disclosure. Even when manifest he is always the stranger."[3]

The path of the solitary is, in the terminology of the eastern Churches, *apophatic* rather than *kataphatic*, an entering into the mystery rather than an explaining of it. This is why the call to solitude is itself mysterious, with little outward manifestation. The solitary is not called to be anything other than a window into God. Any ministry that a solitary undertakes is incidental to the life, not an essential part of it, an overflow from the life of prayer. It is God alone on whom the solitary is centred. The discourses of the desert abbas, the preaching of the wandering Irish monks and of such figures as St Francis spring from the love of God in which they were rooted. St Francis' discourse on 'perfect joy'[4] shows that for him joy lay in being dispossessed and outcast, the sharing of the joy of the crucified.

The misunderstanding encountered by the solitary, the criticism offered by those who see the Christian life as being all about evangelism, or the forming of community, or some other particular activity of care and concern, has to be quietly accepted as part of the cross. The life of the solitary is essentially a hidden life, with little outward manifestation. The purpose of the solitary is to be a focus of God's love, and it is God who is the one who shapes and directs the life of the solitary who must live in total dependence upon God without anxiety. To do this he or she must learn to say no to a great many demands other people make upon time, energy and commitment, and above all to simplify one's life.

This simplification is a matter of making decisions; this way but not that way. But the decisions have a certain inevitability about them. Certain sacrifices have to be undertaken and choices made. It is rather like pruning a tree; in order that the tree may bear good fruit the branches must be pruned. But it is not just the dead and decaying wood that has to go but also good burgeoning shoots, full of possibilities.[5] It is a matter of deciding the priorities in one's life. For the solitary it is God alone.

Solitude is not isolation. There are those who choose isolation, to separate themselves from society. Sometimes they are those who have been wounded by life, sometimes they are those who have chosen to be self-centred and who have refused to open themselves to others. Because their centre is full of self they have no room for God. Those who have God at their centre look not in the mirror of themselves but at God. Charity, in the definition of Thomas Aquinas, is the love of God and of those whom God loves. The true solitary is one who stands at the heart of the world's suffering, at the heart of the cross.

The modern solitary is one who is called to live an ordinary life alongside other people. There may still be those who are called to complete solitude as anchorites, but the medieval hermit, although in many ways a recluse, lived much the same sort of life as his fellow-countrymen.

Common humanity joins us all. The monks of the desert, living on the margins of existence, were aware of the fragility of the common enterprise and of the brevity of human life. When we are weak, then we are strong (2 Cor 12:10), because we do not then rely upon our own strength, but on God alone.

So today's solitary is to be found among other people, in the deserts of daily life, distinguished by no special clothing or manner of life or other singularity. The difference, the separation, is an interior one, invisible to most other people.

One of the ways traditional monasticism expressed its life of solitude was in the separation from all forms of social engagement. Monks were those who had renounced the normal life of local community, of family relationships, of marriage and children. The web of social life was broken, the monk stood alone, without antecedents or dependants. The responsibilities of wife and children which might draw the solitary into social life and away from solitude were renounced. Celibacy became almost a definition of the monastic state, where God alone became the focus and concern, the object of desire.

Yet outside the life of the monasteries the solitary life was led by ordinary lay people. The monastic movement was of course originally a lay movement, the monk's life was a simple lay life with nothing churchy about it. So the call to solitude felt by so many ordinary people today is a return to the original form of the life. Yet celibacy nowadays may not be part of it. There were married hermits in the Middle Ages, a fact that is not widely known because of the belief that being unmarried is somehow a holier state which sets one apart from the rest of us. It is perfectly possible to combine marriage with the solitary life although it can be a demanding vocation, involving the combination of two apparently conflicting claims.

There are different sorts of solitude in marriage. When a relationship has broken down the resulting solitude can be bitter, a real entering into the cross. But this suffering can lead us to the realisation that it is only God who is our ultimate fulfilment, and that our wounds must be joined to Christ's wounds. We can seek the perfection in human life which belongs to God alone. In the joys of the early days of a partnership the couple seek to be everything to each other; only as one grows in experience does one realise that the best marriages are those where each partner has a satisfying and fulfilling life in their own right and does not seek their own justification and value in their partner. That is, that each can give the other space to be a person in their own right, not just as a half of a relationship. All too often a 'happy marriage' can mean one where one of the partners has made most of the sacrifices.

Space for oneself and space for others is all part of the space for God which has to be wrested from one's life. Silence and solitude, the space for God alone, must not be sacrificed but kept in balance. God is the aim and the end. The sacrifices are ours alone to make, not those of other people. But it is essential that one learns to say no to many social invitations and activities, things which all too easily can draw one away from the point to which one is called. This will of course not be understood by most other people; today's world does not value solitude and silence

As has been seen, life in the Egyptian deserts did not involve complete separation from other people, however much solitude was sought. The great abbas and ammas of the desert were those who had encountered their own conflicts and sins, who knew every devious turn of the human heart. This complete freedom from illusion enabled them to act with perfect charity towards others, with compassion for their struggles and with hospitality towards all. That this charity extends to all of creation is shown by the many stories of saints and animals. The animals, lions, gazelles, seals who appear in these stories are aware that here is a man who has no fear or aggression towards them; they accept him as one of themselves who radiates total love.

This perfect charity is the fruit of maturity, but it is the aim of the solitary life. Just as the pursuit of solitude is possible within a coenobitic setting of living with other people, it is likewise not incompatible with an ordinary life of living with others. It is, again, a matter of one's priorities. Charity towards other people is all part of the ascetic struggle towards placing God at the centre of one's life. Charity is the fruit of solitude.

NOTES

1. *Rule of St Benedict*, 1.
2. *Code of Canon Law*, n. 604.
3. Maximus the Confessor (580-662), *Ambigua*, PG 91, 1048-9, quoted in Olivier Clément, 'The Roots of Christian Mysticism', New City 1993.
4. *Fioretti*, chapter 8.
5. I am indebted to Hebe Welbourn for this image.

CHAPTER 9

Discovering solitude

The call to be solitary can gradually unfold itself, but because this call is not generally understood today it can be the cause of distress. Anyone who chooses to be alone is seen to be 'opting out', whether from the usual social occasions or from the present-day Christian scene where the norm is to be involved, to be ministering to others and to be seen to be ministering. Anyone not so involved is regarded as odd, deviant or defective.

Yet the Christian tradition contains many different paths, all of which are ways to God for those who follow them. The task for individual Christians is to discover the path which is the personal and individual way in which they are called; no two people will be led in exactly the same way. There is, as we have seen from the preceding chapters, a long history of Christian solitary life which, although they may not be aware of it, remains an option today for many people, despite the constant emphasis upon activity which current fashion maintains.

Very often the foundation of solitude is laid early in life, even before birth according to the prophet Jeremiah: "Before I formed you in the womb I knew you, and before you were born I consecrated you" (Jer 1:5). There is a moving account in one of Thomas Merton's letters describing the foundations of his solitude in childhood and his uncertainty as to his identity, his nationality or where his home was. He was given solitude at a very early age through the circumstances of his life and the rest of that life was spent in discovering it.

So solitude can haunt us all our days but be felt as something from which we have to fly. The demands are uncomfortable, asking for a total commitment which involves giving up the easier options and the comfortable compromises. Society conditions us against solitude, although it is the first experience of human life, when we are thrust naked and screaming from our mother's womb into an alien world. The infant's need for food and warmth leads to a dependence upon others and gradual socialization. Only in adolescence does one achieve a perception of the self as being separate from one's family and social background, with individual choices to be made. Such a separation can be a very distressing and painful time. For some, like Thomas Merton, the uncertainties of childhood meant that the perception of selfhood and his own separateness arrived early. The usual experience of adolescence is that this separate self seeks a new social milieu, another community of like-minded individuals in which one plays a different role from the one the family expects. Personal solitude, if one is successful in this new socialization, is shunned, as is silence.

When, after much struggle we choose solitude or it chooses us, it may be welcome or unwelcome. The loss of a partner, retirement or redundancy, or other life-crises may be the occasion for a new look at one's life. Familiar support systems, accepted values have crumbled, and one is thrown back upon one's own slender resources. One can seek distraction or one can accept the poverty and need one is experiencing, and enter into the solitude one is given. This may be a new experience or it may be an echo of a call previously heard which returns with greater urgency. Opening the door to solitude does not mean however settling down to a comfortable self-centred existence where other people make minimal demands upon one. To choose the solitude one is given is to choose a desert path where God is the one making demands, demands which have no limits. It is not an easy option.

Until now we may have seen ourselves in the mirror of others' esteem. In solitude there are no mirrors, and one is faced with the painful and painstaking task of deconstructing the mirror images and discovering our true selves. The solitary's path is the reverse of that presented to us by today's consumer society which tells us that we are not fulfilled as people unless we possess this or that desirable object. In solitude there are no goals; any object that appears before us is a desert mirage which disappears as we approach it. We all live in a world of images and idols, familiar and comforting symbols of what we take for reality, objects of worship or desire. These mirages of the desert offer the immediate satisfaction of hunger and thirst while leaving untouched the deeper hunger and thirst, which is for God alone.

The call to solitude, however it manifests itself, is essentially a call to separation in some way from society. The early monks were known as *akathistoi*, the rootless ones, who had chosen to separate themselves from the social milieu of locality and family which placed them in the ancient world. Today, when it is a rare occurrence to remain in the local community where one is born, we all live as rootless people in the deserts of post-industrial society. The separation of today's solitary is most likely to be an interior one, although periods of physical solitude may become necessary, desired but perhaps not always attained. Amma Matrona of the desert said: "It is better to be surrounded by people, and live the solitary life in intention, than to be alone and wish to be with the crowd".[1] Nowadays the call may manifest itself in the first instance as a general distaste and dissatisfaction with what the great majority of people accept as ordinary everyday living. It is both a longing for an unknown good and a feeling of exile from the desired object vaguely perceived. It is an absence, a void.

This sense of absence can be a challenge or it can be an experience of desolation, a profound distaste for one's condition, a boundless desert where there is no consolation. The wells are dry and one's thirst remains unquenched. One may seek distraction, an escape route from this lack of satisfaction, to plunge into the meaningless pleasure-seeking which today's society offers us only too readily. Or one may choose a whole world of illusion to replace the one we thought we had abandoned. There is the feeling that one should have something to show for being a Christian, listening to those who, with the best of motives, seek to draw one from the path of solitude to take part in active works of mercy and join in various social activities. The temptation is to find a role to play, a role which will bring a sense of self-importance, a sense that one is really counting for something in one's Christian life.

The false self that these escape routes construct is the greatest enemy of the solitary. The solitary has no role to play because the search in which she or he is engaged is not one for personal identity but for emptiness, for the meaning of the profound solitude of God. The path, which is unmarked, lies over the abyss of oneself.

Silence recalls us to solitude, it breaks in upon our existence. It is sufficiently rare an experience in the modern world to be cherished. In the 1939-1945 war many serving men had their first experience of silence and solitude in lonely night watches at sea or in the desert, something they had never encountered before. One can be solitary in a crowd of people but silence draws us out into a dimension beyond our existence, beyond human speech. Silence poses the question of our being; this is why it is so often fled from. In silence there is no occupation for our busy ego which has here nothing to feed upon. One is nothing in a vast and empty space, waiting for the unknown.

To wait in silence is to place ourselves in the hands of God. Unlike most experiences in human life we are not in charge, our own skills and competence will not extricate us from the situation. We can only wait. When we wait for a bus or train or plane to arrive there are distractions from the boredom of waiting, but here there is only silence and solitude. Giving ourselves to the silence we discover that silence is not just absence of noise or human speech but that it has a positive pervasive quality. The silence becomes an inward silence.

In the constant verbalisation of twentieth century culture, where every experience has to be described and every description has to be commented upon, we have reached a place beyond all words. In silence one can only listen, allowing it to encompass us. Silence is the gift of solitude. When we possess it we are truly solitary.

The life of the solitary is a silent and hidden life which grows within the busy demanding everyday life we all lead. The old desert fathers spoke much of the importance of the work of the cell, the place of personal solitude. Abba Moses said, "Sit in your cell and your cell will teach you all things".[2] The interior solitude of the solitary is the cell where knowledge of self and knowledge of God enter. Abba Antony said: "Just as fish die if they stay out of water, so do monks when they linger outside their cells in the company of worldly people and are turned away from their intention of quiet. As it is necessary for fish to return to the sea, so must we return to the cell, lest by staying outside we forget our interior watchfulness".[3] Nowadays we have to carry our cell with us, as the snail does, but we should always be prepared to leave it at the demands of charity. It is however the solitary's home, the natural element where we live, and to which we return. Abba Allois of the desert said: "Unless a man says in his heart 'Only God and I exist in this world', he will not find peace".[4] St John of the Cross echoes this in saying that one should live in a monastery as if there were no-one in it but God and oneself.[5]

There is another instructive story from the desert however: Abba Daniel and Abba Ammois were on a journey together. Abba Ammois, missing the peace of his cell, said: "Do you think that some time we shall sit down together in a cell, Abba?" And Abba Daniel replied: "Who takes God away from us? God is with us as we journey and again is with us in the cell".[6]

Someone may object, "This sounds like the old 'garden of the soul' spirituality of fifty years ago. Nowadays we find God in other people's needs rather than in the practice of individual piety." To this we may answer that everyone's path to God is personal and individual, and that while serving other people's needs may be a fulfilling path for some it is not so for those who are aware of being called to solitude. The road of the solitary lies in receiving not giving, in loss rather than in abundance. To live in the desert without reward is a particular calling, and the calling is from God. It is not a path that can be followed by everyone or understood by everyone. In whatever way one is called, whether to the service of others or to solitude, one should be faithful to one's call as it is given.

The Christian solitary exists within the Church, the company of the baptised, and the solitary vocation must be lived out in dialogue with the Christian tradition. The solitary life is prophetic in that it runs counter to the values of the society in which it is lived; such a life has no aim or ambition, no goal of achievement; it is a life lived in obedience to an interior voice.

Such a life is lived with no thought of personal reward. It is a gift to the whole Church, a sign of the transcendence of God. It will be judged in the light of monastic tradition, although the paths which are followed may not be those of historically conditioned monasticism. Living water overflows the channels dug to contain it and new wine requires new wineskins.

Because the path of the solitary seems to run counter to the current view of what constitutes the Christian life or even to the recognised monastic life, the solitary can seem to be a peculiar person. In this identification with those isolated by society the solitary represents the outsider and is a bearer of suffering. The way is the way of the cross, of the Jesus who was identified with the outcast and sinners (Heb 13:13). It is not surprising therefore that there should often be little place within the local church for the solitary, whose path lies rather in the wilderness. In the Bible however it is in the wilderness, outside the camp, that the voice of God is heard.

The life of the solitary is not an easy life, since there are no prescriptions for it and each day must be faced anew. The signs which say "keep in lane" or "when red light shows wait here" are of little relevance to one who is called to strike across country, equipped with a rather inadequate map and a compass one has not yet learnt to trust. From time to time the solitary seeks affirmation, reassurance that the path along which he or she is being drawn is genuine and not an illusion. If one is fortunate enough one may encounter someone of wisdom and insight, one possessed by the Spirit, who may be able to discern the way of the Spirit in the other. She or he may be able to perceive the way which has been travelled up to that point, and perhaps obstacles to further progress. But it is certainly not a time for rules and prescriptions, but of sensitivity to what St John of the Cross calls "the delicate anointings of the Spirit".

Sometimes no guide appears, and one is given no such reassurance. This is a test of faithfulness, of perseverance in the face of doubt and darkness. The early pioneers of the desert of course had no guides. They just went out into the desert, the place of desolation, and got on with it. The hidden work of the cell, combined with the manual labour which was the other half of the work, was their main occupation. One saying compared the cell with "the furnace of Babylon, where the three children found the Son of God, and it is also the pillar of cloud from which God spoke to Moses".[7] The cell, the place of silence and solitude where one encounters God, is the place where illusions are encountered, recognised for what they are, and stripped away, and where there is nothing to distract one from the inner search.

It is the Spirit who guides, whether through the words of another or directly. This direct guidance is the usual path of the solitary, and is something to which great attention must be paid, since it is the only compass bearing that may be available. Each person will be led by a different path; some will have a simple and clear path to tread, others will proceed by making many false turns and errors before the way is clear. All this takes place, not by the extraordinary means of visions and revelations (although such things may possibly occur) but by the ordinary events of one's daily existence.

The hidden life of the solitary is not a world of fantasy or dreams but the place where one encounters God. The solitary is one who is not just alone, but alone with God. "Those with whom God is," says William of St Thierry, "are never less alone than when alone".[8] Entering the desert is not an escape from reality. The desert is a place of simplification, where one's initial ideas of oneself and of God are purified. It is a place of thirst, which will be satisfied only by God. God alone suffices, as St Teresa said. The light of the desert is clear and pure which penetrates into every corner of one's life, even the darkest corners. All must be illuminated and perceived.

NOTES

1. *Vitae Patrum*, V. ii. 14.
2. *Ibid.*, V. ii. 9.
3. *Ibid.*, V. ii. 1
4. *Ibid.*, V. xi. 5.
5. St John of the Cross, *Counsels to a Religious*, 2.
6. *Vitae Patrum*, V. xi. 8.
7. *Ibid.*, V. vii. 31
8. William of St Thierry, *Golden Epistle to the Carthusians of Mont Dieu*, iv.

CHAPTER 10

Practical solitude

Solitary life is not a life of simple self-pleasing, a comfortable retreat from the demands of real life and of other people. Such demands have to be fully met, which is part of the ascesis of the solitary. The self-satisfied life places the individual at the centre. The life of the true solitary places God at the centre. This life refers always to something other than itself, the mysterious unknown.

The solitary life as it is lived today outside a monastic setting is a profoundly ordinary life. It does not differ in outward appearance from the sort of life lived by everyone else; like consecrated bread, it is the hidden and invisible element which makes it different. But it is this hidden life which will be the governing factor, which will demand a total allegiance and to which the rest of our life will be ordered. It is a blank cheque, with no bottom line; the sum to be written upon it is unknown and unspecific. Without this total generosity towards God there will be no progress. Yet it is a life of struggle, not one of peace, since God's ways are not our ways. We learn little by little, and painfully, what is asked of us.

The life of seeking God in solitude is not an easy life. It meets with little understanding from many of our fellow-Christians who have different ideas of what constitutes a Christian life. In order to be faithful to this call we are aware of we have to understand the historical traditions of the solitary life which show us that we are not at all 'odd', but successors in a tradition which is as old as the church itself. This does not mean adopting a particular lifestyle in the medieval manner, but seeking what might be broadly termed a contemplative life in the midst of all the busyness of twentieth-century existence. We do not withdraw from the world but maintain our inner cell of quiet in the midst of all the turmoil of our everyday lives of work and family. This does not mean that one does not have to cultivate one's human relationships. All the elements of this life have to be given full weight; no-one becomes a true solitary at the expense of another human being.

Yet this interior quiet is the place where we encounter God, in solitude and silence. To maintain this place there must be a 'no' as well as a 'yes'. Life must be so arranged that solitude is given full importance in the day; if one is busy that is all the more reason for taking time out to be alone and quiet. With quiet ruling one's life the rush and hassle fall into place and can be taken in one's stride. One is no longer ruled by pressure. When one's life is given wholly to God everything that happens, whether joyful or sorrowful, is to be seen as God's gift. So solitude cannot be seen as a retreat from life, a moving into a sphere of sentimental religiosity, an anodyne refusal of the unpalatable, but as an entering more deeply into the mystery of the cross.

Solitude of course is an interior disposition, which external solitude confirms and strengthens. One can be quite solitary in the midst of a crowd, and one's opportunities for solitude during the day are not necessarily those when one is entirely alone, but times when one's attention is directed inward and away from the distractions which surround us. The mind can go flying about, following one stimulus after another, captive to a dozen things which grab our attention. The secret is to look beyond these things by focussing upon the one point, which is God. If we are seeking God, God is seeking us; it is a relationship which has to be fostered, as human relationships have to be fostered. Like falling in love, it is a process where we are taken beyond ourselves into an unknown world.

As this relationship continues the ideas and concepts with which we began will change. Just as a child in growing up needs clothing of a larger size, so the equipment we begin with will prove insufficient and will have to be discarded. It is a process of moving from security to insecurity, of launching out into the deep and leaving behind the comforts of familiar and well-tried ways. The story of the Bible is one of a people called out of their security to depend upon God alone, and who abandon this dependence for something more tangible, idols of all sorts. All God asks is our yes. God is faithful even if we are not and prefer our own particular idols, whether power, money, sex, our own image of ourselves, or our religious practices. The consumer society is full of idols; we are persuaded that we are not fulfilled as people if we do not possess this or that desirable object or follow this or that pattern of popular culture. Even green politics can become an idol of correct thinking. The solitary is called to stand apart from this sort of pressure, and to discern its distorted nature.

The solitary life is lived in many different ways. There are as many ways to God as there are people. There is no right way or wrong way, but the way God has chosen for you in the situation you have been placed in, which you have to discover. So beware of those who say, "This is the right way" or "That is the right way" (cf. Mt 24:23), for the path for you is the one God has chosen for you personally, which only you will recognise. We are all spiritually deaf and blind and struggle hard against God's demands upon us, clinging to our own familiar possessions. Like the Israelites of old, we are called into the wilderness of God (Deut 8:15).

The desert to which the solitary is called is not a place, but something that must be there below the surface of ordinary human existence. It is nowhere, a place of thirst after God. But to enter this desert one must be aware of the dangers of living in it and to be able to face these dangers. In the monastic tradition a time of preparation was expected, where one learned in the light of God to find all the things in oneself, one's weak spots, one's refusal of grace, that prevent the clear and unequivocal 'yes' to God's call. There must be a journey to a painful maturity and a vision of oneself as naked before God, without the fig-leaves of the social self or the concealments of religious platitudes. The old stories from the desert of the struggles with demons were tales of the struggle with just these alienated aspects of oneself, the things that sought to dominate the personality. The desire for reward, for recognition, for admiration are potent demons, as are the greed for fulfilling one's bodily needs beyond the simple and natural limits, and the desire for stimulation of all kinds which the modern media feed upon. These are some obvious demons to be faced and named.

This is a struggle which continues. It is very easy to become complacent and overlook certain faults in oneself, until perhaps one is brought up short against them by happenings or encounters that reveal them. One has to remain watchful and humble, resting in the centre of one's own humility. Just as the blemishes in one's skin are revealed when one looks into a bathroom mirror in a bright light, so the light of God shining into one's heart can reveal the imperfections there. Where there is no light these things are not seen; without this revealing light one can live in a world of self-created illusion.

The disciplines of solitude will be different for everyone. Maintaining an inner cell of quiet will be a greater struggle for the person with family obligations or for those whose life involves working closely with other people. Here one must make use of the time one is given throughout the day, even if it is only a moment or two, to offer one's life to God. It is like having a compass in one's hand, pointing to the true north. The busyness of life will swing the needle, but it will return again to the same direction. Dramatic gestures are easy, simple faithfulness requires more effort.

Prayer is not so much a matter of specific occasions, forms, words, but a constant orientation towards God which becomes habitual. This is the hidden life which goes on inside the external one which differs little from any other human life except for the hidden thirst for solitude, silence and simplicity, a thirst which it may be possible to quench only intermittently. But if it is possible to arrange one's life so that these things may be enjoyed then one should not hesitate to do so. Even in the rush of the city there are oases of peace; churches may be open, and other places of unexpected silence may present themselves.

If one lives alone solitude is no problem. A regular discipline of prayer and reading can be maintained. But activities are not a measure of our response but one's thirst for God, which may be the greater in privation. The Pharisee in the parable (Lk 18:10) kept all the rules of prayer and good behaviour, fasting and covenanting part of his income to charity. The tax-collector on the other hand, the man of dubious moral standing, asked only for God's mercy. One cannot earn one's salvation; what matters is being aware of one's need for God in one's life. With that need, with that thirst, one gives oneself to God.

Such a gift is a turning-point. One does not suddenly become a better person; in fact all one's faults may now seem darker and darker and more intractable. But from that point the autonomy, the independence so valued in modern life, gives place to a strange feeling of someone else being in control. At first this may be a peaceful experience, like moving from rough water to a smooth-flowing stream. But we soon find that this is not the end of the story but only the beginning. We are just asked to go on saying 'yes' in the face of whatever may happen. There are strange failures, things go wrong, doors close, plans laid carefully come to nothing. It is a time of frustration and struggle. At the point of despair, where one gives up trying to make sense of this disorder, an alternative will appear. A door will suddenly open on a new possibility, a new way forward will present itself. Or the events of one's life suddenly appear in a new pattern, like doing a jigsaw puzzle when the picture begins to appear. From then on listening rather than talking is more important; it is as if something is being said quietly just beyond one's level of hearing, if one can but grasp its meaning. Now and again the old self will want to take over, trying to arrange things in neat orderly patterns to make sense of it all, and wanting to take charge of the situation.

The solitary life must be fed, as all living things must be. Just as an animal, grazing in a field, knows the right things to eat, so the solitary will by interior leadings find the nourishment for the spirit. Reading should not be neglected; the spiritual treasures of the past are available, although it may need some persistence to find them. Public libraries are a resource; most offer a service to obtain books on request. At the back of this book are some suggestions. Many of the spiritual classics were written in another age and in a different religious climate, but the search for God is constant, in any age. The language may be strange but it speaks of the same thing.

Retreats are another resource which should be used, particularly by those who lead a busy and distracted life. If seclusion is sought, many religious houses offer facilities for the private retreatant, with silence and solitude. Longer periods of silence may be possible; one may be able to borrow or rent a cottage in a secluded area. Sometimes the rates are a lot cheaper outside the holiday seasons. There are times when a longer period of seclusion seems necessary, and it should be approached with some care.

This venture into complete solitude is not a holiday, although some recreation may be part of it. It is a way of reassessing one's life and one's priorities, a way of putting down for a period the burdens and cares of one's life in order to pay attention to what is happening within. It is important therefore to leave these burdens and cares behind and not pack them with one's luggage. St Catherine of Siena was told, "Look after my affairs, daughter, and I will take care of yours." So it will be. If there is a telephone in the house, arrange that you may be contacted if necessary at specific times, say between 6 and 7 in the evenings. At other times let it ring, which is a good discipline in detachment!

This time of aloneness is time given wholly to God, unlike one's usual everyday life where the claims of people and things have to be balanced. Take food and other things you need with you, as far as possible, so that the distraction of shopping trips can be avoided. Take plenty of books, spiritual classics that you may not have read or ones that you know and of course a Bible. Take also something lighter for recreational reading; something like a biography is a better choice than a thriller or novel which is apt to stimulate the imagination too much. Television watching should also be strictly limited for the same reason. But set aside some time for recreation; as the story from the desert has it, the bow that is kept constantly strung soon breaks.

Silence and simplicity should govern the day. As Aelred of Rievaulx directed his sister: "You sit, you keep silence, you suffer things to happen."[1] Your occupation should be varied; after an hour or two spent in reading or prayer, do some housework or cooking or go out for a walk. Feel comfortable with your rhythm, which is merely the frame-work within which the Spirit is at work in you. The aim is a balanced existence, where the body and the spirit are given an equal share. But the point of your seclusion is to allow the voice of God to be heard in the silence without the distraction of other cares. It is a time of spiritual progress, though you may only be aware of a curious blankness. Just accept all that comes to you.

Antony said, "The one who sits in solitude has escaped from three wars, hearing, speaking and seeing; he has only one battle, that is the battle of his own heart."[2] You may be drawn into periods of darkness and suffering as certain elements of your life from the past or present bring them-selves to your attention. These have to be accepted and brought into the light of God, who searches all hearts. You are being shown things in yourself that you would rather not know about; your wounds have to be brought to God and united with the wounds of Christ. Our wounds are not healed but glorified; as St John of the Cross says, the wounds due to another cause have become the wounds of love.[3] Or as Bernard of Clairvaux says, we enter into the life of God through the wounded side of Christ. This is the profound mystery of our union with God, the suffering that we share.

The fruit of this period in total solitude should be a stabilisation or affirmation of your vocation, a complete commitment, an unequivocal yes. This yes is entirely hidden, without the wearing of any external token such as a religious habit, but it is an acknowledgement of having been touched by the hand of God. It may be that more than one period of total solitude may be necessary to work through all that is called for; the stabilisation of one's aims however in this initial period may lead to a reordering of one's life so that solitude is put firmly at the centre of things. The whole of one's life will become prayer.

This total solitude is not a necessary part of the solitary life but, rather like the possession of a bicycle, it enables one to travel more rapidly across the country. Here one can encounter many things nakedly, without the distractions with which daily life is inevitably filled. Paradoxically, these distractions are of course part of the discipline of prayer and do not exist in one compartment of life while 'prayer' exists in another. It is with the whole of human life that God is concerned, and it is the vocation of the solitary to draw all human life to God.

NOTES

1. Aelred of Rievaulx, *De Institutione Inclusarum.*
2. *Vitae Patrum*, V. ii. 2.
3. St John of the Cross, *Living Flame of Love*, 2nd redaction, Stanza II, 7.

CHAPTER 11

The prayer of the solitary

If the vocation of the solitary is the primary monastic vocation, then some consideration of monastic traditions of prayer may be expected to cast some light upon the way solitaries pray. St Paul says (Rom 8:26) that prayer is the work of the Holy Spirit praying within us, which means that it is as much a question of listening as of talking, a constant dialogue taking place between God and our individual, imperfect and faithless selves. Each person's prayer is peculiar to themselves, a personal language which may take some time to discover, even a lifetime. This is the sort of prayer which forms the life of the solitary.

This is not to say that the prayer of the solitary is 'protestant' compared with liturgical prayer, which is 'catholic'. Barsanuphius, a sixth-century Egyptian monk who lived in Gaza, writes:

> "The hours and psalmody are customs of the Church and are wisely established to reconcile all men (in prayer) as well as to unite the many in communities. Those who live in sketes [the solitaries] do not read the hours or psalmodise, but occupy themselves in solitude by working with their hands, reading and meditation and from time to time stand up to pray."[1]

From this it is clear that the tradition of prayer for solitaries was different from that of the coenobitic tradition. The Christian solitary prays always within the Church, and within the monastic solitary tradition, but this tradition is not that of the daily Office of the Benedictine rule, which is widely taken as the norm, despite the many current modernisations by monastic communities. The Benedictine Office is a highly structured affair, designed for the uniting of the coenobitic community, communal prayer spread over the day, based on ancient Jewish prayer: "Seven times a day I praise thee" (Ps 119:164), and using ancient Jewish psalms. Some modern solitaries do in fact use the Benedictine Office for their own regular prayer, but this presupposes being able to set aside regular times throughout the day, which is seldom compatible with a life of secular work and family life. The modern solitary, living in the deserts of daily life, has to integrate prayer and work in the way that the early desert monks managed to do.

For work was an essential ingredient of those early lives, in their search to support themselves. The day was spent weaving mats and baskets, which would be sold in the market to provide bread and salt and other bare necessities. Even in the Pachomian monasteries, which were coenobitic work-communities, the communal prayer or *synaxis* was always accompanied by work; each monk would be provided with steeped palm-leaves for plaiting during the prayers.

In this way the monk was identified with the labouring poor, those who depended solely upon God for their daily bread. St Benedict accords great place to manual labour in his Rule, and says that the tools of the monastery must be regarded with the same reverence as the vessels of the altar.[2] When they have to labour in gathering the crops "Then are they truly monks, when they live by the labour of their hands, as did our fathers and the Apostles."[3] To live by the work of one's hands is a tradition that has tended to disappear from 'official' monasticism with the idea that the monk lives upon the offerings of the faithful, who belong to the working 'world'. The monk, by contrast, is one whose work is prayer, who lives a contemplative life, an idea which owes more to the classical ideal of the philosopher expounded by Plato than to primitive monastic tradition. Monastic reformers, such as St Benedict and the early Cistercians have always emphasised the place of manual labour, the work of the hands. The monk's work, as the Cistercian Thomas Merton remarked, is 'worldly' rather than 'churchly'.

Work itself then is an ascetic tool in the life of union with God. Work is a human necessity, common to all (Gen 3:19). It is an objective task, something to be done, a burden laid upon us. It is not an evil necessity, something which has to be got through in order that we may have the leisure to do other things. This is the classical attitude, where the philosophers employed slaves to do the work while they dwelt in *otium*, leisured contemplation of eternal truths. The disciplines of work are the same whether they are those of simple manual labour or of the highly complex work by which we earn our living in today's society. The disciplines are easier to see in manual labour perhaps, and simple tasks such as housework or gardening can be a corrective to the over-intellectualisation of much modern work. Work must be done well, and the task must be completed. The work itself imposes the discipline; our part is to organise it and carry through its efficient completion.

Working with other people too is an ascetic discipline. When St Benedict described the monastery as "a school of the Lord's service"[4] he was presupposing that those in the coenobium had a common aim. Today's solitary will probably be working with those who do not have this aim, and who may well have a different attitude to work. To be faithful in this situation is a test of one's prayer. Barsanuphius, who was quoted earlier, gives the following answer to a young man who complained that he was busy all day long and prevented from remembering God: "It happens sometimes that a man has heard much about a certain city, but when he comes there he does not realise that it is the same city about which he had heard so much. It is the same with you, brother. All day long you remember God without being aware of it. The meaning of obedience and the remembrance of God is precisely to have a commandment and try to keep it, as coming from God".[5] The good habits and disciplines of work are reflected in the work of our prayer, our listening to God.

The solitary is one who is called to a life of prayer. This does not mean spending long periods upon one's knees (a most uncomfortable posture for prayer anyway). The prayer of the solitary is a constant orientation towards God, like the compass needle which always returns to the true north. The discipline of this life is intended to produce the single-mindedness which places God as the centre of our being and the aim of all our activity. It is a life of union with God, a deep and still centre beneath the storms which rage above.

This union is seldom achieved overnight. As Thomas Merton put it, "It is a matter of growth, deepening, and an ever greater surrender to the creative action of love and grace in our hearts."[6] Just as two people who are in love can spend long periods of time together without speaking a word, so it can be in prayer. But at other times one should feed one's prayer with reading, of the Bible and of the writings from the past of those who have travelled this way before. The old method of *lectio divina* involved meditative reading of the Bible and other writings, a slow consideration or chewing over of what is revealed in a reading of the text. The guide in such matters is the Spirit, both in what is chosen and in what is revealed. Such a habit helps to establish both a foundation and a climate for one's life of prayer, the continual interior dialogue with God.

Such a life of prayer is the quiet centre in ordinary everyday life. "He prays unceasingly" says Origen, "who combines prayer with necessary duties and duties with prayer. Only in this way can we find it practicable to follow the directive of Paul to pray always (1 Thess 5:17). It consists in regarding the whole of Christian existence as a single great prayer. What we are accustomed to call prayer is only a part of it".[7]

One approaches God with empty hands, bringing nothing but ourselves and our own poverty and need of God. To be aware of our profound nothingness in the face of God, is to acknowledge God's mystery and immensity. Listening rather than talking is our task. The prayer of the solitary does not consist in many words. Abba Macarius said: "Much speaking is not necessary. All we need is to hold out our hands and say, 'O Lord, what you will and what you please, so be it.' But if trials and struggles attack you, you must say, 'God help me!' for God knows what is needful for us."[8]

This sort of prayer is woven into daily life, a constant awareness of our own dependence upon God. This is not a childish abnegation of responsibility for our own welfare but a lively awareness of what we lack.

The simplicity of the solitary's prayer does not involve intellectual concepts or beautiful literary expressions. The little fourteenth century English classic 'The Cloud of Unknowing', written for a solitary, describes this simple prayer as "this blind outreaching love to God himself, this secret love pressing upon the cloud of unknowing",[9] the darkness which is between us and God. The imagination will be busy filling this darkness with ideas, memories, plans for the day, all of which must be ignored and cast into the darkness. The attention must be focussed on a point beyond the mind's noise. "Beat away," continues the author of the 'Cloud', "at this cloud of unknowing between you and God with that sharp dart of longing love. Hate to think about anything less than God, and let nothing whatever distract you from this purpose".[10] The work of prayer is "fundamentally a naked intent, none other than the single-minded intention of the spirit directed to God alone. I call it 'single-minded' because in this matter the perfect apprentice asks neither to be spared pain, nor to be generously rewarded, nor indeed for anything else but God's own self. So he cares not whether he be grieved or glad, but only that the will of the one whom he loves be fulfilled. And so it is that God is perfectly loved for himself, and above all his creation".[11]

It will be clear that this sort of prayer does not depend upon times and places, but is eminently suited to modern life. The 'single-minded intention' can be held on to throughout the day, whatever it is that our work or other activities engage us in. As with any pair of lovers, meetings are sometimes necessary; the sharp dart of longing love must come to our consciousness. But there are many occasions for this when we are alone, although perhaps not physically alone. Travelling to work, going for a walk, eating one's lunch, can all be part of a time of inner silence. The secret is never to waste time but always to make use of perhaps only a minute or two to glance at God. And so our whole life will be woven into our prayer.

Such prayer can never be a commodity. One's relationship to God is not a trading partnership, earning one's keep by piling up petitions and intercessions for the needs of the world. This would be, as the author of 'The Hermitage Within' says, turning our encounters with God into business meetings.[12] Prayer is never for anything but only that God's love, will and purposes be done in the world, and to pray is to open oneself to this love, will and purpose. So often we will not let God be God but spend our time asking for what we think the world needs, placing our own ideas, in other words ourselves, before what God is wanting of us. God teaches the heart, says the French writer de Caussade, not by means of ideas but by pains and contradictions.[13] Giving up our own ideas is the final surrender.

This disengagement from our own will is the last stage in a long progress. As we have seen, one begins without knowing one's real self, perceiving oneself as a reflection in the mirrors of other people's regard. As we learn to leave the hall of mirrors, the mirages of particular images dissolve and one begins to see one's true face. Until now much of this will have been hidden by the *eidoles*, the false images and illusions which are the only things which have been visible so far. The demons of the desert were the personifications of these false images, the temptations and deceptions of the human heart which have to be unmasked and encountered. As the desert monks knew, this was a long and painful struggle in which the chief weapon is humility, that willingness to regard oneself as nothing, a beginner and learner in God's school.

There are no easy roads along this way, no short cuts, no special offers or cut-price bargains. To gain the pearl of great price one has to give all one has without, like Ananias and Sapphira (Acts 5:1) keeping back a portion for oneself. One will be filled with God only in proportion as one empties oneself. This is a long road which will be travelled for many years; progress will depend upon the desire of the traveller and pilgrim, and the purification of this desire. It is all too easy to spend time in wayside taverns and other pleasurable diversions; the task is one of discovering all the obstacles in the path which prevent us from journeying onwards.

There is no other way than that of discovering the demons of our own heart, and unmasking them. This is a stage of finding our own true identity. The face which gazes out on us from the mirror is one full of blemishes and faults which we will perceive more and more clearly in the light of God, in whom there is no deception. When we can see ourselves as God sees us, then we are living in the truth.

But beyond the mirror a further journey lies ahead. "He must increase, but, I must decrease" (Jn 3:30). There is a saying of Antony to the effect that the perfect monk is one who does not know he is praying, which points to the disappearance of one's own face as one lives a life of union with God. This is a hidden life where the 'me' has dissolved. This union of course has been there from the beginning, from the first call to be solitary; now it has deepened.

The prayer of the solitary is a matter of continual simplification, the lesson we learn from wandering up blind alleys in search of satisfaction for the demands of the ego to be fed, fleeing from the no-thingness of God. Simplicity is unity, a capacity for being one-pointed and resting entirely in the providence of God. Prayer will then be a matter of the opening of windows into God, a simple perception of God's presence in the world. This meeting-point is also a standpoint, a place from which one cannot be moved, a place of vision unclouded by the world's propaganda and the techniques of the persuasion industry. It is a place of safety and of freedom.

The world needs solitaries, those who are able to stand outside the political, religious or social systems of the world and cast a cold eye upon them. God's mysterious transcendence of which the solitary is a bearer is always beyond the world's systems. But God is always at work in the world, and the solitary is both witness and channel for the peace and justice of God which the world rejects.

NOTES

1. *Writings from the Philokalia on Prayer of the Heart*, tr. E. Kadloubovsky and G.E.H. Palmer, Faber and Faber 1951, p. 351.
2. *Rule of St Benedict*, 31.
3. *Ibid.*, 48.
4. *Ibid.*, Prologue.
5. *Writings from the Philokalia*, p. 364.
6. Thomas Merton, *The Asian Journal*.
7. Origen, *On Prayer*, 12. PG11, 452.
8. *Vitae Patrum*, III. 207.
9. *The Cloud of Unknowing*, tr. Clifton Wolters, Penguin Books, ch. 9.
10. *Ibid.*, chapter 12.
11. *Ibid.*, chapter 24.
12. *The Hermitage Within, A Monk,* Darton, Longman & Todd, 1977, p. 87.
13. J. P. de Caussade, *Self-Abandonment to Divine Providence*, 2.2.

Contemplative living

The path of the solitary, whose essential separation from society means that it is a very different one from the way most people recognise, lies in hidden and unknown places. It is like climbing a mountain with ropes and an ice-axe, hacking out, as one goes, places to put one's feet, rather than a gentle stroll along the plain upon well-trodden paths. For although the landmarks of the spiritual life have been noted by the great travellers of the past, it is always an adventure into new country. It is the same world one has always known but one has somehow become a stranger to it, a stranger and pilgrim upon the earth. The sense of separation which may always have been there has been realised.

The solitary has always to live upon the margins, with the questions and uncertainty, the unknowing, and to be content to live there. The world rejects this sort of living, seeking always answers and certainties, black and white. The solitary, however, has to rest in uncertainty and insecurity, in a world without labels, never settling down in a particular place or into systematic answers and explanations which draw lines round the mysterious presence of God in the created world. God is present in the dynamic and in the mysterious interior dialogue which continues. Always what is partly grasped and understood is overwhelmed by that which is larger. There are no answers which are adequate.

As a bearer of transcendence the solitary points to the mystery at the heart of life. Because it is beyond words this mystery has no explanation, it just is. The solitary too shares in God's essential incomprehensibility, not being understood by those among whom he/she dwells, or even by himself/herself. The one who dwells on the margins is the one who has discarded the accumulations of the world's values, and has another currency. The margin-dweller is the one who has no possessions in the land.

The solitary is the one who has learned by painful paths to live without props, the props supplied by other people, whether the props of self-affirmation, emotional support or the reassurance that one is going the right way. Even reliance upon the religious practices which at one time have provided such comfort must go. One leaves the broad green paths for those which are steep and rough. Only the emptiness, the no-thingness, is real.

In this place of incomprehension the solitary must be content, not understanding her/his own solitariness, presenting no face to the world, assuming no recognisable identity, not even any name with which the world can come to terms. To the world, the solitary remains an enigma, an outsider with no recognisable identity.

The solitary is a sign of contradiction, and a sign which will be spoken against. God is the centre of existence and the life of the solitary is lived as a total response to God. Such single-mindedness will be incomprehensible to those who have not been grasped by the utter transcendence of God, and who will feel uncomfortable or challenged by such a response. The world rejects this otherness of God, the ultimate mystery which defies naming or labelling, or being turned into a commodity. Such a God challenges the things which people live by, their values and their priorities. The world's response to such a challenge is rejection and crucifixion. The way of the solitary is a following of the crucified one, and a bearing of the world's anguish.

The path of the solitary is silent and hidden. The solitary has no use and no ministry, no visible sign, not even a vision of himself/herself as solitary, a quiet self-satisfaction at one's position. We remain always imperfect, failures by the world's standards, cast upon the divine mercy, and thirsty for God's grace, simply waiting with empty hands.

The being of the solitary, as bearer of mystery, is itself mysterious. We desire nothing except God, we have nothing except that which we are given. As Paul puts it (2 Cor 4:7), the treasure we are given is contained in vessels of common clay, not in anything glorious. Common clay is easily broken, humble and unvalued.

The guidance of the solitary is most usually an interior one, which one in time learns to trust. Certain actions, certain interpretations, are given with an insistent force which is self-authenticating. If such things are refused they will often return in another form, until they are made perfectly clear.

The life of the solitary is one of abandonment to the providence of God, learning to be dependent upon God alone and not upon one's own competence. It is not without struggle that this attitude is learned. Like Jacob at the ford, we struggle with an unknown adversary in the darkness. One is really being asked for the sacrifice of one's own ideas, one's own feelings of competence, of always being master/mistress of the situation, which a certain degree of accomplishment in one's own field has given one. What must go is the sense of one's own worth, which the practice of humility may have reduced considerably already, so that one may feel that one is prepared for anything. But now even the ordinary ability to manage one's own life, the everyday competence to handle situations, may be taken away. One is bobbing about like a cork in the sea, with no sense of direction or purpose. Everything is taken away, sometimes bit by bit, and sometimes in a way that makes one say, like St Teresa, "It is no wonder Lord that you have so few friends when you treat them like this!"

By such painful paths one learns that God's ways are not our ways, and that the 'cloud of unknowing' in which we are enveloped is to teach us this fact. We learn to stop struggling like a child in its mother's arms, demanding to be put down to walk on its own feet, and allow ourselves to be peacefully carried the way of God's intentions for us. What these intentions are will be revealed in due course, not in any way that can be grasped, but in the things that happen. Doors will open into new possibilities, decisions made for us.

The sacrifices are ours alone to make. No one becomes a true solitary at the expense of another human being, and human and personal relationships have to be cultivated. Catherine of Siena was told, "Look after my affairs daughter, and I will take care of yours". This places God at the centre of all things; the self-sufficiency of the solitary as practised by the old desert monks is an expression of dependence upon God alone and not on the support and regard of other people. This God-centredness enabled them to act with perfect charity towards others. If the life of the solitary is not filled with joy, not just happiness which is an ephemeral thing in human life, it is not filled with God.

For St Francis perfect joy was an identification with the crucified. The cross is the place of peace and reconciliation. The solitary stands at the heart of the struggle, as a channel of God's peace and unity. The world is a place of conflict; the solitary has not opted out of the human struggle but stands at the heart of it. What more solitary place than the cross! The cross is the mysterious saving presence of God at the heart of the created world.

The solitary has no identity and seldom any recognisable ministry. The vocation of the solitary is to silence, poverty and emptiness, things which are strange to the modern world. The solitary life is prophetic in this running counter to the values of the society in which it is lived. Such a life has no aim or ambition, no goal of achievement; it is a life lived in obedience to an interior voice. In a society where everything is measured by its cash value or by its usefulness, the life of the solitary is both useless and unproductive.

Possessing nothing, with empty hands, the solitary is called to a life of prayer. Prayer today is so often seen as a matter of gathering intercession lists; prayer must be useful and God must be recruited to bind up the wounds of the world. The mystery of God's purposes must yield to our importunities. The solitary on the other hand seeks simply to enter the life of God: "Why speak at length?" says Gregory of Sinai (fourteenth century), "Prayer is God, who works all things in all people." Solitude is not for anything, but a sharing in the solitude of God.

Yet in a mysterious and hidden way the solitary contemplative life bears fruit. There is in the eastern tradition the idea of 'spiritual parenthood', the blossoming and fruit-bearing of a life yielded wholly to God. Through such a life God speaks to many hearts. What the fruit may be is known only to God. Such spiritual parenthood is only possible when the individual 'I' has disappeared; as in the story of the Transfiguration (Mt 17:8), the disciples see no-one, but only Jesus.

The traditions of the solitary life are built up by those who live such a life, as paths are made by those who walk them. To the solitary life only God calls. Those who in each successive generation hear this call and obey it are those who bear the burden of God's transcendent otherness, and whose paths lie in another direction from the busy highways and supermarkets of the world. Out there somewhere in the distance, where the roads run out, on the cliff-face, there is a small solitary figure with an ice-axe.

Further reading:
a brief selection

Early Desert Monks

Sayings of the Desert Fathers – the Alphabetical Collection, tr. Benedicta Ward, Mowbray 1975/83

Lives of the Desert Fathers, tr. Norman Russell, Mowbray 1980/88

The Desert of the Heart: Daily Readings with the Desert Fathers, (ed.) Benedicta Ward, DLT 1988

The Desert a City, Derwas J. Chitty, Basil Blackwell 1966

Athanasius, *Life of Antony*, translated from Latin, R.T. Meyer 1950, reprint Paulist Press, USA 1993

Pachomian Koinonia, 3 vols., Cistercian Publications, Kalamazoo, Michigan USA 1980

The Conferences of John Cassian, tr. Boniface Ramsey OP, 3 vols., Cistercian Publications, Kalamazoo, Michigan USA 1994

Frère Ivan, *Desert and the City, A quest for interiority in the footsteps of the Desert Fathers*, St Pauls, Slough 1993.

Marcel Driot, *Fathers of the Desert, Life and spirituality*, St Paul Publications, Slough 1992.

The English solitary tradition

The following are available in a modern translation as Penguin Classics:

The Cloud of Unknowing, tr. Clifton Wolters.

The Ladder of Perfection, Walter Hilton, tr. Leo Sherley-Price.

The Fire of Love, Richard Rolle, tr. Clifton Wolters.

Revelations of Divine Love, Julian of Norwich, tr. Clifton Wolters.

Ancrene Wisse: Guide for Anchoresses, (ed.) H. White.

Aelred of Rievaulx, De Institutione Inclusarum, translated from Latin, J. Ayto and A. Barratt, *Early English Text Society*, Oxford University Press 1985

Hermit of Finchale: Life of St Godric, (ed.) Rice, Pentland Press 1994

R.M. Clay, *Hermits and Anchorites of England*, London 1912 gives a remarkable account of the solitary life in England in the Middle Ages. It is not an easy book to get hold of.

William of St Thierry, *The Golden Epistle*, translated from Latin, W. Shewring. Sheed & Ward, USA 1980. Also with introduction by J.M. Dechanet OSB, Cistercian Publications, Kalamazoo, Michigan USA

Peter F. Anson, *The Call of the Desert,* SPCK 1964. A history of the solitary call in the religious life and of notable hermits.

The most profound writer on solitude in modern times is Thomas Merton (1915-1968). There are five essays on the solitary life in 'Contemplation in a World of Action', published in Great Britain 1971 by George Allen & Unwin. There are three further essays in 'The Monastic Journey', published in Great Britain in 1977 by Sheldon Press, and 'Notes for a Philosophy of Solitude' in 'The Power and Meaning of Love', Sheldon Press, 1976, a selection of essays from 'Disputed Questions', published in USA by Farrar, Straus and Giroux, 1953.

The Hermitage Within, A Monk, DLT 1977/80, by a French Solitary, is highly recommended.

Ordinary People as Monks and Mystics: lifestyles for self-discovery, Marsha Sinetar, Paulist Press USA 1986 is a non-Christian approach to the solitary life, based on the idea of 'social transcendence'. A very interesting book.

Solitude, Anthony Storr, Fontana Paperbacks 1989. A psychologist's case for solitude, claiming that the capacity to be alone is a sign of maturity.

Further information about the Fellowship of Solitaries, founded in 1990, can be obtained from Eve Baker at Coed Glas, Talgarth Road, Bronllys, Brecon, Powys, LD3 0HN.